My
Internet
for Seniors

Michael Miller

que®

800 East 96th Street,
Indianapolis, Indiana 46240 USA

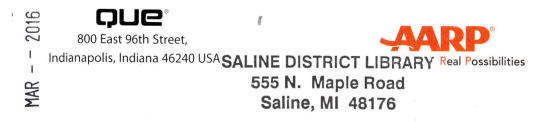

My Internet for Seniors

ISBN-13: 978-0-7897-5743-2
ISBN-10: 0-7897-5743-5

Library of Congress Control Number: 2015956949

Printed in the United States of America

First Printing: February 2016

Trademarks

All terms mentioned in this book that are known to be trademarks or service marks have been appropriately capitalized. Que Publishing cannot attest to the accuracy of this information. Use of a term in this book should not be regarded as affecting the validity of any trademark or service mark.

Warning and Disclaimer

Every effort has been made to make this book as complete and as accurate as possible, but no warranty or fitness is implied. The information provided is on an "as is" basis. The author, AARP, and the publisher shall have neither liability nor responsibility to any person or entity with respect to any loss or damages arising from the information contained in this book.

Special Sales

For information about buying this title in bulk quantities, or for special sales opportunities (which may include electronic versions; custom cover designs; and content particular to your business, training goals, marketing focus, or branding interests), please contact our corporate sales department at corpsales@pearsoned.com or (800) 382-3419.

For government sales inquiries, please contact governmentsales@pearsoned.com.

For questions about sales outside the U.S., please contact international@pearsoned.com.

Editor-in-Chief
Greg Wiegand

Acquisitions Editor
Michelle Newcomb

Marketing Manager
Dan Powell

Director, AARP Books
Jodi Lipson

Development Editor
Brandon Cackowski-Schnell

Managing Editor
Kristy Hart

Senior Project Editor
Betsy Gratner

Copy Editor
Geneil Breeze

Indexer
Erika Millen

Proofreader
Debbie Williams

Technical Editor
Jeri Usbay

Editorial Assistant
Cindy Teeters

Cover Designer
Mark Shirar

Compositor
Nonie Ratcliff

Contents at a Glance

Table of Contents

3 Choosing and Using a Web Browser   **37**

4 Browsing and Searching the Web   **65**

12   Sharing Your Photos Online   215

13   Exploring Your Genealogy Online   239

20 Staying Safe Online **323**

Glossary **343**

Index **351**

About the Author

Michael Miller is a prolific and popular writer of more than 150 nonfiction books, known for his ability to explain complex topics to everyday readers. He writes about a variety of topics, including technology, business, and music. His best-selling books for Que include *My Social Media for Seniors*, *My Facebook for Seniors*, *My Windows 10 Computer for Seniors*, *My Samsung Galaxy S6 for Seniors*, *My Google Chromebook*, *Easy Computer Basics*, and *Computer Basics: Absolute Beginner's Guide*. Worldwide, his books have sold more than 1 million copies.

Find out more at the author's website: **www.millerwriter.com**

Follow the author on Twitter: **@molehillgroup**

About AARP and AARP TEK

AARP is a nonprofit, nonpartisan organization, with a membership of nearly 38 million, that helps people turn their goals and dreams into *real possibilities*™, strengthens communities, and fights for the issues that matter most to families such as healthcare, employment and income security, retirement planning, affordable utilities, and protection from financial abuse. Learn more at aarp.org.

The AARP TEK (Technology Education & Knowledge) program aims to accelerate AARP's mission of turning dreams into *real possibilities*™ by providing step-by-step lessons in a variety of formats to accommodate different learning styles, levels of experience, and interests. Expertly guided hands-on workshops delivered in communities nationwide help instill confidence and enrich lives of people 50+ by equipping them with skills for staying connected to the people and passions in their lives. Lessons are taught on touchscreen tablets and smartphones—common tools for connection, education, entertainment, and productivity. For self-paced lessons, videos, articles, and other resources, visit aarptek.org.

Dedication

To my six favorite grandkids—Alethia, Collin, Hayley, Jackson, Judah, and Lael.

Acknowledgments

Thanks to all the folks at Que who helped turn this manuscript into a book, including Michelle Newcomb, Greg Wiegand, Brandon Cackowski-Schnell, Betsy Gratner, Geneil Breeze, and technical editor Jeri Usbay. Thanks also to the good folks at AARP for supporting this and other books I've written.

Note: Most of the individuals pictured throughout this book are of the author himself, as well as friends and relatives (and sometimes pets). Some names and personal information are fictitious.

We Want to Hear from You!

As the reader of this book, *you* are our most important critic and commentator. We value your opinion and want to know what we're doing right, what we could do better, what areas you'd like to see us publish in, and any other words of wisdom you're willing to pass our way.

We welcome your comments. You can email or write to let us know what you did or didn't like about this book—as well as what we can do to make our books better.

Please note that we cannot help you with technical problems related to the topic of this book.

When you write, please be sure to include this book's title and author as well as your name and email address. We will carefully review your comments and share them with the author and editors who worked on the book.

Email: feedback@quepublishing.com

Mail: Que Publishing
           ATTN: Reader Feedback
           800 East 96th Street
           Indianapolis, IN 46240 USA

Reader Services

Register your copy of *My Internet for Seniors* at quepublishing.com for convenient access to downloads, updates, and corrections as they become available. To start the registration process, go to quepublishing.com/register and log in or create an account.* Enter the product ISBN, 9780789757432, and click Submit. Once the process is complete, you will find any available bonus content under Registered Products.

*Be sure to check the box that you would like to hear from us to receive exclusive discounts on future editions of this product.

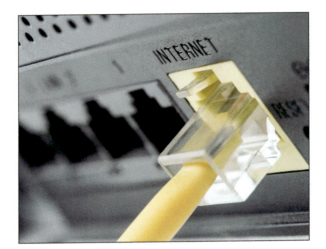

In this chapter, you learn how the Internet works, and how to choose the right type of Internet connection for your home.

→ What the Internet Is—And How It Works

→ Examining Different Types of Internet Connections

→ Installing Internet Service

Choosing an Internet Service Provider for Your Home

Whether you have a desktop or notebook/laptop computer, a tablet, or a smartphone (or all of the above!), to get the most out of your devices, you need to connect them to the Internet. The Internet provides access to all sorts of fun and useful content and services, from news and weather reports to the latest movies and TV shows.

This means you need to have some sort of Internet connection in your home. Fortunately, many companies are willing and eager to connect your home (and your devices) to the Internet. It's just a matter of choosing which service you want and then getting it installed.

What the Internet Is—And How It Works

Before we get into all the details about connecting to the Internet, let's take a moment and discuss just what this Internet thing is in the first place.

If you're new to the Internet, keep one thing in mind: The Internet isn't a thing. You can't touch it or see it or smell it; you can't put it in a box and buy it. The Internet is like the huge power grid that provides electricity to homes across the country—it exists between the points of usage.

So, if the Internet isn't a physical thing, what is it? It's really more simple than you might think; the Internet is nothing more than a really big computer network— that is, a bunch of computers connected together. In fact, it's a computer network that connects other computer networks, or what some would call a "network of networks."

Just being connected to the Internet, however, really doesn't accomplish anything. It's much the same as having electricity run to your home—that wall outlet doesn't do anything until you plug something into it. The same thing is true with the Internet; the Internet itself just kind of sits there until you plug something into it that takes advantage of it.

Understanding Internet Service Providers

When you connect to the Internet to visit a website, send an email, or chat with other users, you're connecting your computer or smartphone to hundreds of millions of other computers—and the information that resides on all those other computers. But before you can contact those other computers, you first have to gain access to the Internet.

Since your computer does not connect directly to the Internet, you instead connect to a company that serves as an *Internet service provider* (ISP)—that is, a company that is directly connected to the Internet and provides Internet service for you and other consumers. Your computer connects to the ISP, the ISP connects to the Internet, and thus you are connected to the Internet.

Connecting to Your ISP

When you sign up for Internet service from an ISP, the Internet itself comes into your home via a wire or cable and connects to a device called a *modem*. This little black box then connects either directly to your computer or to a wireless network router, so you can share the connection with all the computers and wireless devices in your home.

Broadband modem ——

It works like this:

(1) Your personal computer or other device connects to your home network's wireless router.

(2) The router connects to the modem supplied by your ISP.

(3) The modem connects to your ISP.

(4) Your ISP connects to the Internet.

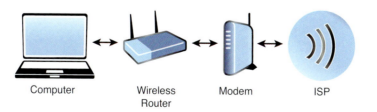

Computer   Wireless   Modem   ISP
                Router

Your computer is now connected to the Internet, through your ISP.

>>>*Go Further*

SERVERS AND ADDRESSES

Everything you access on the Internet is hosted on a computer; these computers are called *servers* because they serve information and services to users. The Internet itself comprises hundreds of millions of individual servers, each connected by a high-capacity data backbone. This backbone routes data and communications from one server to another at near-instantaneous speeds.

Each server and device connected to the Internet is identified by a specific address, called an *Internet Protocol (IP) address*. An IP address is specified using dot-decimal notation with a series of numbers divided by dots, like this: **123.45.678.9**

The Internet uses an underlying networking technology called *Transmission Control Protocol/ Internet Protocol (TCP/IP)* to manage data transmission and communications between Internet servers. To contact a given server, your web browser or other software specifies an IP address; the communication is then routed to the Internet server that uses that specific IP address.

All this technical stuff happens in the background, so you don't have to worry about it much if at all. But you can see how complex the technology is that drives the Internet; a lot goes on behind the scenes when you visit a website or send an email!

Examining Different Types of Internet Connections

As discussed, the first step in going online is establishing a connection between your computer and the Internet. When you're connecting from home, you need to sign up with an ISP to provide your home with a connection to the Internet.

The biggest ISPs today are your local/national cable and telephone companies. Comcast/Xfinity, AT&T, Verizon, and more typically offer Internet service using a variety of technologies. You might even get a discount if you bundle your Internet service with your cable TV or phone service.

Most ISPs today offer various types of *broadband* access. As opposed to the older *dial-up* Internet access, which used your regular phone line to connect, broadband Internet comes via a dedicated connection and offers much faster speeds. In addition, broadband Internet is always on, so you can go online any time you want.

Several different flavors of broadband connections are available today. You can find broadband Internet connections using digital subscriber line (DSL), cable, fiber optic, and even satellite technologies. We look at each of these separately.

DSL

DSL is a phone line–based technology that comes from your landline telephone company and operates at broadband speeds. Unlike old-fashioned dial-up access, DSL doesn't use your existing voice line, but rather piggybanks on it. That is, the phone line comes into your house into a splitter; the voice line goes to your phone, as usual, but the DSL line taps off that and goes to the Internet modem.

As noted, DSL stands for *digital subscriber line*; it's a high-speed digital connection. Download speeds are typically in the 3 Mbps to 10 Mbps range, although both slower and faster connections are sometimes available.

DSL connections are "always on" and independent of your regular phone service. Most providers offer DSL service for $20 to $50 per month. Look for package deals that offer a discount when you subscribe to both Internet and phone services.

It's Not All Good

Data Caps

It isn't all about speed. Some ISPs employ "data caps" for customers who download too much data, effectively throttling their use or charging extra for excessive data usage. Others offer different subscription plans with different data usage levels. As always, it pays to check the fine print on these items before you sign up.

Cable

Another popular type of broadband connection is available from your local cable company. Broadband cable Internet piggybacks on your normal cable television line, providing speeds ranging anywhere from 2 Mbps to 150 Mbps range, depending on the provider.

In general, cable Internet is faster than DSL, although you pay for that speed. Budget (low-speed) plans can be had from some cable companies for as little as $15/month. Plans offering higher-speed service can run up to $75/month. Your cable company probably has several different plans available. And, as with DSL, look for package deals from your cable company, offering some sort of discount on a combination of Internet, cable, and (sometimes) digital phone service.

Fiber Optic

The newest type of broadband connection comes via fiber optic cable. Fiber optic (sometimes called *FiOS*) is the fastest type of connection available today, with some ISPs offering both download and upload speeds of a blazing 1 Gbps. Pricing isn't bad either, typically in the $45 to $100 range. Fiber optic service is most often offered by local telephone companies.

In the home, the fiber optic cable connects to a modem-like device called an optical network terminal (ONT) that splits the signal to provide a combination of Internet, television, and telephone services. You typically connect the ONT to your wireless router or PC via an Ethernet cable.

Unfortunately, fiber optic Internet isn't as widely available as DSL or cable. You may or may not have fiber optic service available in your area; while coverage is improving, it's still hit or miss.

In the United States, fiber optic Internet service is available in limited areas through Verizon, Level 3 Communications, Frontier, AT&T, and others. Contact your local provider to see what's available.

Satellite

If you can't get DSL, cable, or fiber optic Internet in your area, you have another option—connecting to the Internet via satellite. Any household or business with a clear line of sight to the southern sky can receive digital data signals from a geosynchronous satellite at speeds between 5 Mbps and 15 Mbps.

The largest providers of satellite Internet access are HughesNet (www.hughesnet.com) and Exede (www.exede.com). (Hughes also developed and markets the popular DIRECTV digital satellite system.) Satellite systems enable you to receive Internet signals via a small dish that you mount outside your house or on your roof. Fees range from $50 to $110 per month.

Dial-Up

If you don't have access to broadband Internet or if you simply want a lower-priced alternative, you can still connect via a much slower dial-up connection. This is how everyone used to connect, before broadband Internet became common. A dial-up connection dials in to an ISP via your existing telephone line, like you're making a phone call.

Still, if you have broadband Internet available, go that route. Dial-up connections are slow (limited to just 56 Kbps, tops) and hijack your phone line while you're connected, and they're just not that practical in today's world of image-heavy websites and streaming audio and video. Dial-up should be the connection of last resort. (And if you already have a dial-up connection from the old days—through a service such as AOL, for example—switch to broadband as soon as you possibly can.)

Comparing Different Types of Connections

Now that you know a little bit about all the different types of home Internet service, let's compare what's available. Know, however, that you probably won't have all options available in any given location. In fact, many people find they have a single option available, from either their cable or telephone (DSL) company. Still, Table 1.1 lists what to expect.

Table 1.1   Home Internet Connections

	Dial-Up	Satellite	DSL	Cable	Fiber Optic
Download speed	56 Kbps	5 Mbps–15 Mbps	500 Kbps–25 Mbps	2 Mbps–150 Mbps	25 Mbps–1 Gbps
Upload speed	56 Kbps	1 Mbps–3 Mbps	384 Kbps–6 Mbps	512 Kbps–10 Mbps	15 Mbps–1 Gbps
Always on?	No	Yes	Yes	Yes	Yes
Average monthly cost	$15–$30	$40–$150	$20–$50	$15–$75	$45–$100

The costs detailed here are the basic monthly subscription costs for the Internet service itself. In addition, you may be asked to pay a monthly rental cost for the broadband modem or gateway device. An up-front installation fee may also be required.

That said, you may qualify for discounted rates if you pay an entire year in advance or if you bundle your Internet service with cable television or phone services. As always, it pays to shop around.

(And remember, the upload/download speeds—as well as the monthly fees—differ significantly from ISP to ISP, and even between plans at a given ISP.)

>>>Go Further
MEASURING CONNECTION SPEEDS

Internet connection speeds are measured in *bits per second*, or bps. A thousand bits per second is notated as Kbps; a million bits per second is Mbps; and a billion bits per second is Gbps. Obviously, the faster the connection the better—especially for watching online video and listening to online music.

Older dial-up connections are limited to just 56 Kbps and have largely been supplanted by faster broadband technologies. DSL connection speeds approach 25 Mbps, cable Internet can get to 150 Mbps, and the newer fiber optic connections can reach all the way up to 1 Gbps. You typically pay more for faster connections. (Your ISP may offer several levels of service, charging more for faster speed.)

Also know that the speed you get for data coming downstream is typically faster than the speed available for sending things back upstream. That is, your download speed (for receiving email, viewing websites, watching videos, and the like) will be faster than your upload speed (for sending email, uploading videos to YouTube, and such). That's probably okay, as you'll be doing a lot more downloading than uploading.

Installing Internet Service

Installing Internet service in your home isn't difficult. In general, it involves connecting a cable from your ISP to a broadband modem and then connecting that modem to a wireless network router.

If you're dealing with your cable or telephone company, chances are they already have the wiring or cabling run into your house or apartment. (Remember, DSL service piggybacks on your existing phone line, and cable Internet uses your existing cable connection.) It's then a matter of running another cable from the appropriate wall outlet to the modem.

If this is a brand spanking new installation, your ISP may need to run wiring or cabling to your home, and possibly through a wall or two to get to where you want it. That's obviously more involved than just connecting to an existing outlet.

As to who does the installation, it all depends. Some people choose to install things themselves, using an installation kit provided by their ISP. Others prefer to let the ISP (again, typically your cable or phone company) do the installation for them, typically for a fee.

All that said, unless you're a big do-it-yourself person and technically astute, you probably want to let the ISP install your service, even if there's a small fee involved. That's what they get paid for, and they know what they're doing.

Home Networks

Learn more about connecting to a home wireless network in Chapter 2, "Connecting to the Internet—At Home or Away."

Install with a Modem and Wireless Router

If you're okay with handling the technical stuff, many ISPs let you install your own Internet connections. You need the necessary equipment (including that provided by the ISP) and a line run to your house from your ISP. The process is similar for all types of broadband connections.

We start by examining the most common type of installation, where you connect the Internet signal to a wireless network router.

1. Connect the appropriate cable from the wall jack to the broadband modem. With cable, fiber optic, and satellite Internet, you'll probably use a coaxial cable, like the kind you connect to your TV. With DSL, you'll most likely use a standard phone cable.

2. Connect one end of an Ethernet cable to the appropriate port on the modem.

3. Connect the other end of the Ethernet cable to the appropriate port on your wireless router. This may be labeled "Internet," "WAN," or "Input," or may simply be one of the available Ethernet ports on the back of the device.

4. Follow the instructions for your router to connect your PC either via Ethernet or wirelessly.

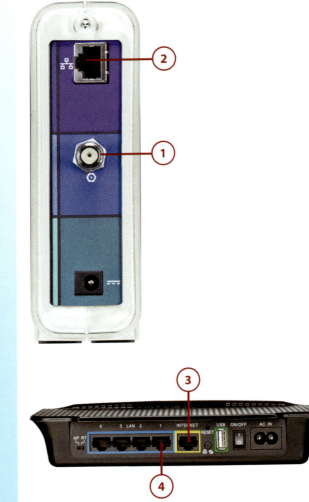

5) Connect the modem to a power source.

6) Power up the router.

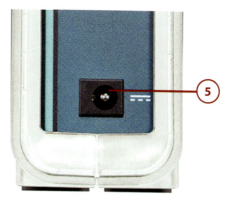

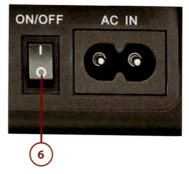

Install with an Internet Gateway

Some ISPs provide a combination modem and router, often called an *Internet gateway* device. If you get this combo box, you don't need a separate wireless router; the wireless networking functionality is built in to the gateway. All you have to do is run the DSL, cable, or fiber optic line to the gateway device; then the Internet signal is automatically broadcast over a wireless network. It's a much simpler installation.

Internet gateway

1 Connect the appropriate cable between the wall jack and the Internet gateway. With cable, fiber optic, and satellite Internet, you'll probably use a coaxial cable, like the kind you connect to your TV. With DSL, you'll most likely use a standard phone cable.

2 Follow the instructions for your gateway device to connect your PC either via Ethernet or wirelessly.

3 Connect the Internet gateway to a power source.

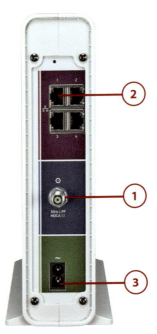

Connecting to the Internet—At Home or Away

To connect to the Internet, you must have an available Internet connection and a device capable of connecting. That device can be a personal computer (Windows or Mac), smartphone, or tablet. Your connection can be in your own home or anywhere that offers a public Wi-Fi hotspot.

Connecting to a Home Network

Let's start by examining what you have to do to connect to the Internet connection in your home. We'll assume you have an Internet connection available and that you have a wireless home network installed, as discussed in Chapter 1, "Choosing an Internet Service Provider for Your Home."

Your home network is a private network, meaning that you need to know the name of the network (also called a Service Set Identifier, or *SSID*) and the network's password (also called a *network security key*).

Connect via Ethernet

The instructions here are for connecting your computer wirelessly. Most desktop and laptop/notebook computers can also connect via a wired connection. Just connect an Ethernet cable between an Ethernet port on your wireless router or Internet gateway and a similar port on your computer. Your computer should automatically recognize the network and connect to it and the Internet.

Connect with a Windows 10 Computer

Assuming your computer has built-in Wi-Fi capability, enable the computer's Wi-Fi and then follow these steps.

1 In the notification area of the taskbar, click the Connections icon to display the Connections panel. If no network is currently connected, the Connections icon should be labeled Not Connected—Connections Are Available.

2 Click your wireless network; this expands the panel for this network.

3 To connect automatically to this network in the future, check the Connect Automatically box.

4 Click Connect.

Connect Automatically

When you're connecting to your home network, it's a good idea to enable the Connect Automatically feature. This lets your computer connect to your network without additional prompting or interaction on your part.

(5) When prompted, enter the password for your network.

(6) Click Next.

(7) When the next screen appears, click Yes to allow your computer to be discovered by other PCs and devices on your home network. You're now connected to your wireless router and should have access to the Internet.

One-Button Connect

If the wireless router on your home network supports "one-button wireless setup" (based on the Wi-Fi Protected Setup technology), you may be prompted to press the "connect" button on the router to connect. This is much faster than going through the entire process outlined here.

Connect with a Windows 8/8.1 Computer

Connecting in Windows 8 and 8.1 is slightly more cumbersome, due to the nature of that operating system.

(1) From the Start screen, press Windows+C to display the Charms bar.

(2) Click or tap Settings to display the Settings panel.

(3) Click or tap the Wi-Fi ("Available") icon to display a list of available networks. Your network should be listed here.

(4) Click or tap your wireless network; the panel for this network expands.

5 Check the Connect Automatically box to connect automatically to this network in the future.

6 Click or tap Connect.

7 When prompted, enter the password for your network.

8 Click or tap Next.

9 When the next screen appears, click Yes to connect with other PCs and devices on your home network. (This lets you share pictures, music, and other files with other computers connected to your home network.) You're now connected to your wireless router and should have access to the Internet.

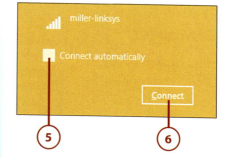

Connect with a Windows 7 Computer

Windows 7 is an older operating system but still used on many computers today.

1. Click the Network icon in the notification area of the Windows taskbar. This displays a pop-up window that lists all available Wi-Fi networks.

2. Click the item for your home network. The area for the selected item expands.

3. Check the Connect Automatically option.

4. Click Connect to display the Connect to a Network dialog box.

5. Enter your network password into the Security Key box.

6. Click OK. You're now connected to the network and the Internet.

Connect with a Mac Computer

Connecting with an Apple computer, running the Mac OS, is similar to connecting with a Windows PC—if not a little simpler.

1. Click the Wi-Fi menu icon to display a list of available networks.

2. Click your network from this list.

3. When prompted, enter the password for your network.

4. Check the Remember This Network option.

5. Tap Join. You're now connected to the network and can use the Internet.

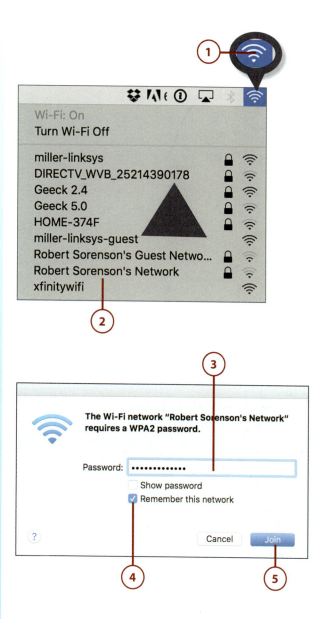

Connect with an Apple iPhone or iPad

When you first want to use your iPhone or iPad on your home network, you need to connect manually. After that, your device should connect automatically when you're within range of your network.

1. Tap Settings to display the Settings screen.

2. Tap Wi-Fi to display the Wi-Fi screen.

3. Make sure that Wi-Fi is switched "on." Your device automatically searches for and displays all available Wi-Fi networks.

4. Tap the name of the network you want to connect to.

5. When prompted, enter your network's password.

6. Tap Join. You're now connected to the network and the Internet.

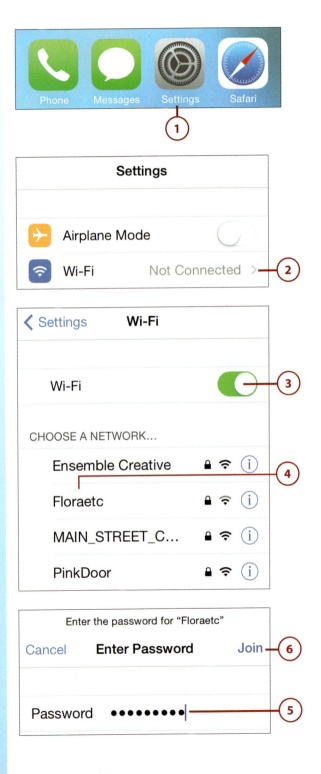

Connect with an Android Smartphone or Tablet

Connecting with an Android device is similar to connecting with an Apple device. Note that the connection process may differ slightly from one type of phone to another; these instructions are for a Samsung Galaxy S6.

(1) Swipe down from the top of the screen to display the notification panel.

(2) Tap the Wi-Fi Networks Available notification *or*...

(3) Tap and hold the Wi-Fi icon to display the Wi-Fi screen.

(4) Tap the name of your home network to display a panel for that network.

(5) Use the onscreen keyboard to enter the network's password into the Password box. (Tap Show Password if you want to see the actual characters as you type; otherwise, you just see dots.)

(6) Tap Connect. You're now connected to the network and can start using the Internet.

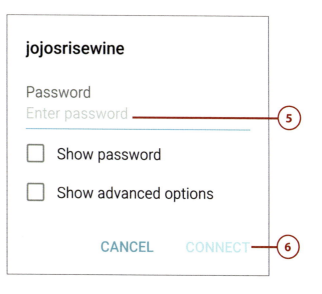

Connecting to a Public Wi-Fi Hotspot

Thanks to the growing embrace of Wi-Fi technology, you can also connect to the Internet when you're away from home. Many coffeehouses, restaurants, hotels, and public spaces offer wireless Wi-Fi Internet service, either free or for an hourly or daily fee.

Hotspot

A *hotspot* is a public place that offers wireless access to the Internet using Wi-Fi technology. Some hotspots are free for all to access; others require some sort of payment.

When you're near a Wi-Fi hotspot, your computer or mobile device should automatically pick up the Wi-Fi signal. Make sure that your device's Wi-Fi functionality is turned on; then follow the instructions specific to your device.

Wi-Fi

Wi-Fi (short for *Wireless Fidelity*) is the consumer-friendly name for the IEEE 802.11 wireless networking standard. Most of today's wireless networks are Wi-Fi networks and use Wi-Fi-certified products.

Connect with a Windows 10 Computer

Microsoft's latest operating system, Windows 10, makes it easy to connect your notebook PC to any public Wi-Fi hotspot. When you're near a Wi-Fi hotspot, your PC should automatically pick up the wireless signal. Just make sure that your computer's Wi-Fi adapter is turned on (it should be, by default) and then get ready to connect.

① On the taskbar, click the Connections button to display the Connections pane.

② You now see a list of available wireless networks. A public network appears with a small warning icon that looks like an exclamation mark inside a shield. (That's because public networks aren't as secure as private ones.) Click the network to which you want to connect.

③ This expands the section for that network; click Connect to connect to the selected hotspot. (If this is a hotspot you visit frequently, you can also check the Connect Automatically option; otherwise, leave this unchecked.)

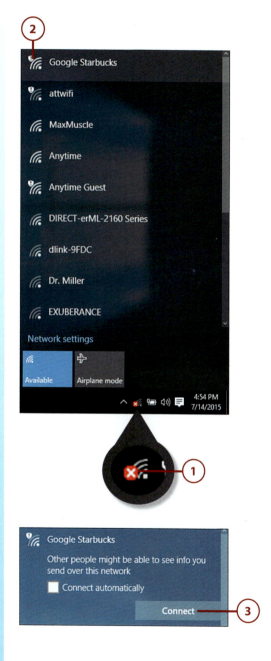

4 If the hotspot has free public access, you can now open your web browser and surf normally. If the hotspot requires a password, payment, or other logon procedure, Windows should automatically open your browser and display the hotspot's logon page. Enter the appropriate information to begin surfing.

Connect with a Windows 8/8.1 Computer

Connecting to a public hotspot with a Windows 8/8.1 PC is similar to connecting to your home network—but with no password required.

1 From the Start screen, press Windows+C to display the Charms bar.

2 Click or tap Settings to display the Settings panel.

3 Click or tap the Wi-Fi icon. (If there are Wi-Fi networks nearby, the icon should be labeled Available.) A list of available wireless networks displays.

4 Click or tap the hotspot to which you want to connect to expand the panel.

5 Click Connect to connect to the selected hotspot.

6 If the hotspot has free public access, you can now open your web browser and surf normally. If the hotspot requires a password, payment, or other logon procedure, Windows should open your browser and display the hotspot's login page. Enter the appropriate information to begin surfing.

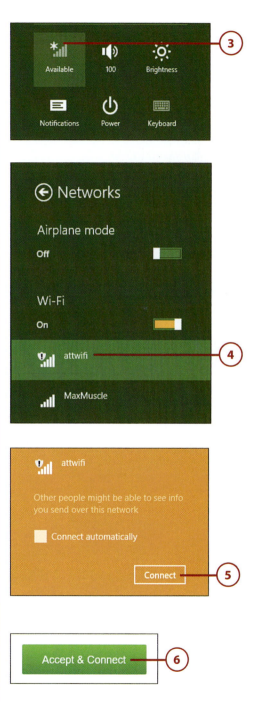

Connect with a Windows 7 Computer

If you have an older notebook PC running Windows 7, you can still connect to public Wi-Fi hotspots.

① Click the Network icon in the notification area of the Windows taskbar. This displays a pop-up window that lists all available Wi-Fi networks.

② Click the hotspot you want to connect to. The area for the selected item expands.

③ Click Connect.

④ If the hotspot has free public access, you can now open your web browser and surf normally. If the hotspot requires a password, payment, or other logon procedure, open your browser and you see the hotspot's login page. Enter the appropriate information to begin surfing.

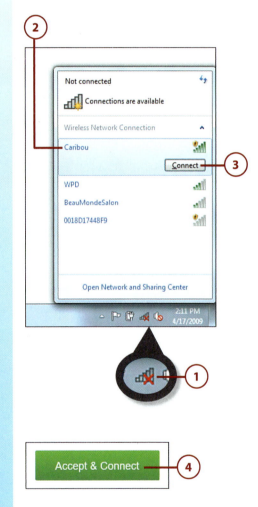

Connect with a Mac Computer

All Apple notebooks have built-in Wi-Fi that makes it easy to connect to any public hotspot.

1. Click the Wi-Fi menu icon to display a list of available wireless hotspots.

2. Click the desired hotspot from this list.

3. If the hotspot has free public access, you can now open your web browser and surf normally. If the hotspot requires a password, payment, or other logon procedure, open your browser and you see the hotspot's login page. Enter the appropriate information to begin surfing.

Connect with an Apple iPhone or iPad

It's equally easy to connect your iPhone or iPad to a public Wi-Fi hotspot.

1. Tap Settings to display the Settings screen.

2 Tap Wi-Fi to display the Wi-Fi screen.

3 Make sure that Wi-Fi is switched "on." Your device automatically searches for and displays all available Wi-Fi networks.

4 Tap the name of the hotspot you want to connect to.

5 If the hotspot has free public access, you can now open your device's web browser and surf normally. If the hotspot requires a password, payment, or other logon procedure, open your browser and you see the hotspot's login page. Enter the appropriate information to begin surfing.

Settings

✈ Airplane Mode

📶 Wi-Fi   Not Connected >

2

3

❮ Settings   **Wi-Fi**

Wi-Fi

CHOOSE A NETWORK...

DIRECT-erML-216...   🔒 📶 ⓘ

Google Starbucks   📶 ⓘ

4

Accept & Connect   **5**

Connect with an Android Smartphone or Tablet

Connecting to a Wi-Fi hotspot is easy with any Android phone or tablet. We use the Samsung Galaxy S6 as an example.

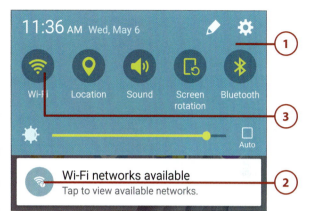

(1) Swipe down from the top of the screen to display the notification panel.

(2) Tap the Wi-Fi Networks Available notification *or…*.

(3) Tap and hold the Wi-Fi icon to display the Wi-Fi screen, with Wi-Fi networks listed in descending order of signal strength. Open networks (those that don't require a password) have a basic icon without a padlock.

(4) Tap the hotspot to which you want to connect.

(5) If you're connecting to a public network, you may see a panel for that network warning that information sent over this network may be available to others. This is normal with most public hotspots and nothing to be concerned about. Tap Connect to connect to the network.

6 If the hotspot has free public access, you can now open your device's web browser and surf normally. If the hotspot requires a password, payment, or other logon procedure, open your browser and you see the hotspot's login page. Enter the appropriate information to begin surfing.

It's Not All Good

Public Hotspot Safety

As you might suspect, public networks are not as secure as those private networks you need a password to access. Because anyone can access a public network, it's possible for malicious users to intercept the signals sent from your computer or device to sites on the Internet. That means you probably shouldn't be sending sensitive information from a public hotspot; save your online banking or shopping for when you're at home on a private connection.

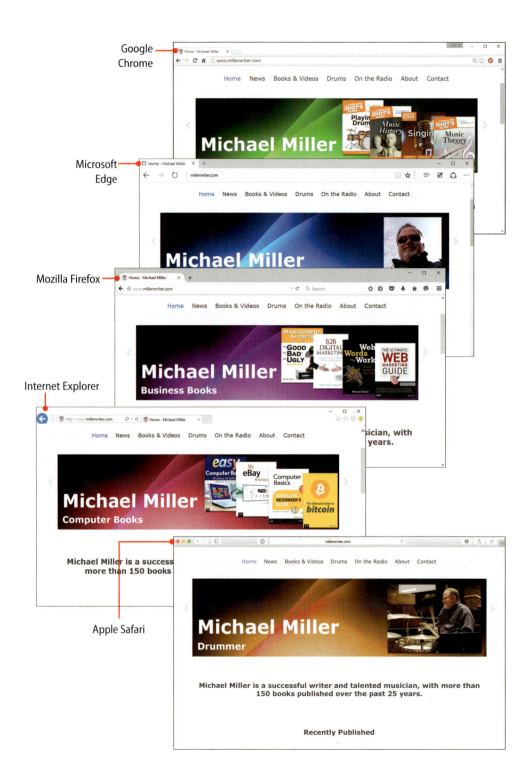

Google Chrome

Microsoft Edge

Mozilla Firefox

Internet Explorer

Apple Safari

3

Choosing and Using a Web Browser

The Internet is made up of many different parts that work alongside each other over the global network—email, social networks, text and video chat, and the like. The most popular part of the Internet is the World Wide Web—what we call the Web, for short.

Sites on the Web—called *websites*, of course—contain all sorts of information and services, and make possible just about everything we do online today. Billions of web pages are interlinked with one another, criss-crossing back and forth like some sort of global spider's web. (Hence the name.)

You access the Web with a piece of software called a *web browser*. There are several web browsers you can use; it's your choice.

Comparing Web Browsers

As noted, you access sites and pages on the Web with a web browser. All web browsers today are free and can be downloaded from their respective websites.

Table 3.1 details the most popular browsers and where to find them.

Table 3.1   Web Browsers

Browser	Publisher	Download Website	Available for These Operating Systems
Chrome	Google	www.google.com/chrome/browser/	Windows XP, Windows Vista, Windows 7, Windows 8/8.1, Windows 10, Mac OS X, Linux, Chrome OS
Edge	Microsoft	www.microsoft.com/microsoft-edge (included with Windows 10)	Windows 10
Firefox	Mozilla	www.mozilla.org	Windows XP, Windows Vista, Windows 7, Windows 8/8.1, Windows 10, Mac OS X, Linux
Internet Explorer	Microsoft	windows.microsoft.com/internet-explorer	Windows XP, Windows Vista, Windows 7, Windows 8/8.1, Windows 10
Safari	Apple	www.apple.com/safari/ (included with Mac OS X)	Mac OS X

All these web browsers support *tabbed browsing*, which enables you to open multiple web pages at the same time, all in their own individual tabs. All browsers also let you store shortcuts to your favorite web pages as bookmarks or favorites. And all keep a history of web pages you've visited, which makes it easy to return to recently viewed pages.

That said, each browser in this list has its own unique look, feel, and operation. Some load certain web pages faster than others; some are easier to use than others. While you can certainly stick with the browser that came preinstalled on your computer, you can also check out the other browsers and see which best fits the way you browse the Web.

In the following sections we look at how to use each of these popular web browsers.

Using Microsoft Edge for Windows 10

Microsoft Edge is the newest browser in this bunch, included in Microsoft's new Windows 10 operating system. (And only with Windows 10; at this writing, Edge is not available for any other operating system.) It replaces Microsoft's older and aging Internet Explorer browser.

As the newest browser available, it sports the latest flat design and a state-of-the-art feature set. It's fast and full-featured and is rapidly becoming the browser of choice for a majority of Windows 10 users.

Go to a New Web Page

Microsoft Edge, like all web browsers, has an Address box into which you enter the address for any web page you want to visit. (Naturally, you can also click a link on any web page to go to that other page, as well.)

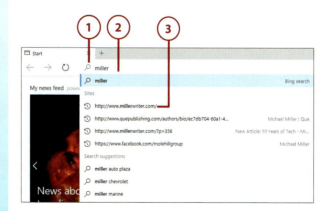

1 Click near the top of the browser window to display the Address box.

2 Start to type a web page address into the Address box.

3 As you type, Edge displays a list of suggested pages (and a few suggested web searches, too). Click one of these pages or finish entering the web page address and press Enter.

4 To return to the previous web page, click the Back (left arrow) button beside the Address box.

5 To reload or refresh the current page, click the Refresh button.

4   **5**

← → ↻

>>>Go Further
LARGER TYPE

If the text on a given web page is too small for you to read, Microsoft Edge lets you zoom in to (or out of) the page. Click the More Actions (three dots) button, go to the Zoom section, and click + to enlarge the page (or click – to make the page smaller).

Work with Tabs

Most web browsers, including Microsoft Edge, let you display multiple web pages as separate tabs, and thus easily switch between web pages. This is useful when you want to reference different pages or want to run web-based applications in the background.

1 To open a new tab, click the + next to the last open tab.

2 To switch tabs, click the tab you want to view.

3 Click the X on the current tab to close it.

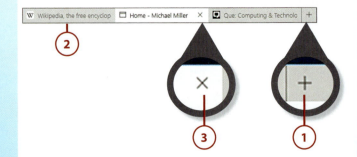

Save Favorite Pages

All web browsers let you save or bookmark your favorite web pages. In Microsoft Edge, you do this by adding pages to the Favorites list.

1. Navigate to the web page you want to add to your Favorites list and then click the Favorites (star) icon in the Address box.

2. Click to select the Favorites tab.

3. Confirm or enter a name for this page.

4. Click the Add button.

Revisit History

To view a list of pages you've recently visited, click the Hub (three-line) button and select the History (timer) tab. Click the page you want to revisit.

Return to a Favorite Page

To return to a page you saved as a favorite, open the Favorites list and make a selection.

1. Click the Hub button to display the Hub panel.

2. Click the Favorites (star) tab to display your Favorites list.

3. Click the page you want to revisit.

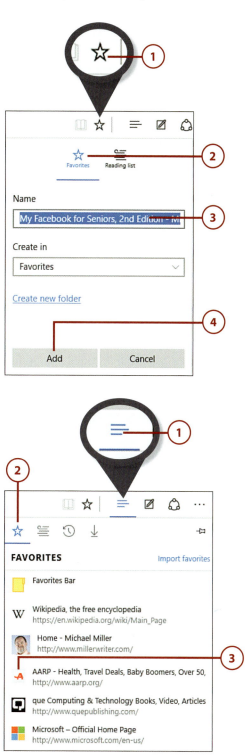

Favorites Bar

For even faster access to your favorite pages, display the Favorites bar at the top of the browser window, beneath the Address bar. Click the More Actions button and select Settings to display the Settings page; then click the Show the Favorites Bar control "on."

Browse in Private

If you want to browse anonymously, without any traces of your history recorded, activate Edge's InPrivate Browsing mode in a new browser window. With InPrivate Browsing, no history is kept of the pages you visit, so no one can track where you've been.

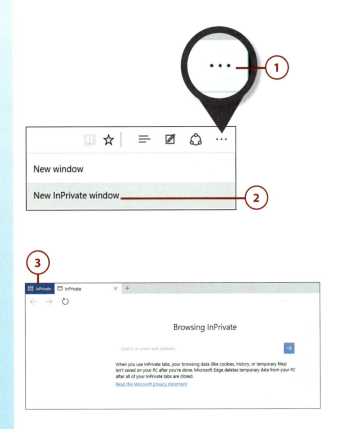

1. Click the More Actions button.
2. Select New InPrivate Window.
3. A new InPrivate Edge window opens, ready to accept any web page address you input.

Browse in Reading View

Some web pages are overly cluttered with advertisements and other distracting elements. You can get rid of these visual distractions by activating Edge's Reading view—which also increases the size of the text on the page, making it even easier to read.

In Reading view, all the unnecessary items are removed, so all you see is the main text and accompanying pictures. In addition, the onscreen text is significantly larger in Reading view, and there's more "white space" all around. The result is, perhaps, the best way to view web pages if you have even slight vision difficulties.

1 Navigate to the page you want to read; then click the Reading View button on the Edge toolbar.

2 This removes the unnecessary elements, increases the text size, and makes reading easier. Click the Reading View button again to return to normal view.

Configure Browser Settings

You can configure many options within Edge to personalize your web browsing experience.

(1) Click the More Actions button.

(2) Click Settings to display the Settings pane.

(3) Configure the desired option.

New window

New InPrivate window

Zoom   — 100% +

Find on page

Print

Pin to Start

F12 Developer Tools

Open with Internet Explorer

Send feedback

Settings

SETTINGS

Choose a theme

Light ⌄

Show the favorites bar

⬤ Off

Import favorites from another browser

Open with

⦿ Start page

◯ New tab page

◯ Previous pages

◯ A specific page or pages

Open new tabs with

Top sites ⌄

Using Internet Explorer

Internet Explorer (IE) is Microsoft's older web browser. It was included with every version of Windows from Windows 95 through Windows 8.1. (It's also included with Windows 10, but not set as the default browser.)

Go to a New Web Page

Use IE's Address bar to enter the address for any web page you want to visit.

① Click within the Address bar and begin entering a web page address.

② As you type, IE displays a list of suggested pages. Click one of these pages or finish entering the web page address and press Enter.

③ To return to the previous web page, click the Back (left arrow) button beside the Address bar.

④ To reload or refresh the current page, click the Refresh button.

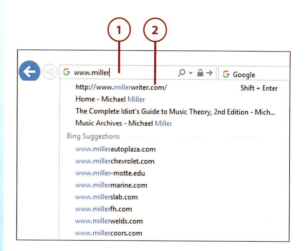

>>>Go Further

LARGER TYPE

To enlarge the text on any given web page, click the Tools icon and then select Zoom. You can click to Zoom In or Zoom Out of the page, or select a zoom factor from 50% to 400%.

Work with Tabs

Like Edge, IE is a tabbed browser. You can load different web pages into different tabs and then easily switch from one page/tab to another.

(1) To open a new tab, click New Tab next to the last open tab.

(2) To switch tabs, click the tab you want to view.

(3) Click the X on the current tab to close it.

Save Favorite Pages

Internet Explorer lets you save your favorite web pages in a Favorites list.

(1) Navigate to the web page you want to add to your Favorites list and then click the Add to Favorites (star) icon in the top-right corner of the browser window.

(2) Click the Add to Favorites button to display the Add a Favorite dialog box.

(3) Confirm or enter a name for this page.

(4) Pull down the Create In list and select a folder to store this favorite. (If you don't pull down this list, you save the web page in the main Favorites folder.)

(5) Click the Add button.

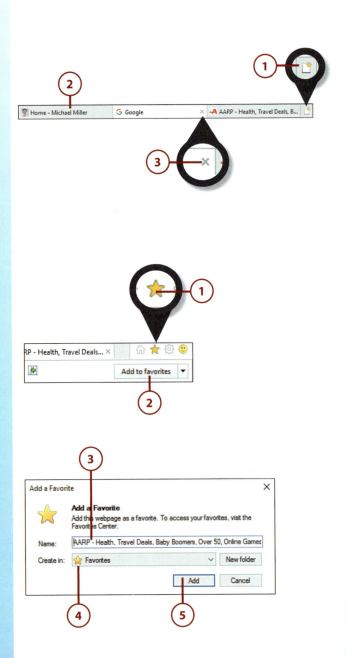

Revisit History

To view a list of pages you've recently visited, click and hold the Back button and then click History.

Return to a Favorite Page

To return to a page you saved as a favorite, open the Favorites list and make a selection.

1 Click the View Favorites button.

2 Click the Favorites tab.

3 Click the page you want to revisit.

Favorites Bar

For even faster access to your favorite pages, display the Favorites bar at the top of the browser window. Right-click next to the row of tabs and then check Favorites Bar.

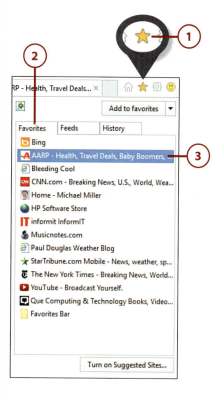

Browse in Private

IE offers the same InPrivate Browsing mode found in Microsoft Edge. InPrivate Browsing lets you browse anonymously, with no history kept of the pages you visit.

1. With IE running in normal mode, right-click the Internet Explorer icon on the Windows taskbar.

2. Click Start InPrivate Browsing.

3. A new InPrivate IE window opens, ready to accept any web page address you input.

Configure Browser Settings

Within Internet Explorer you can configure many options to personalize your web browsing experience.

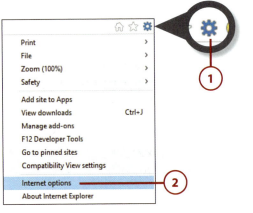

1. Click the Tools button.

2. Click Internet Options to display the Internet Options dialog box.

3 Select the appropriate tab to configure related options.

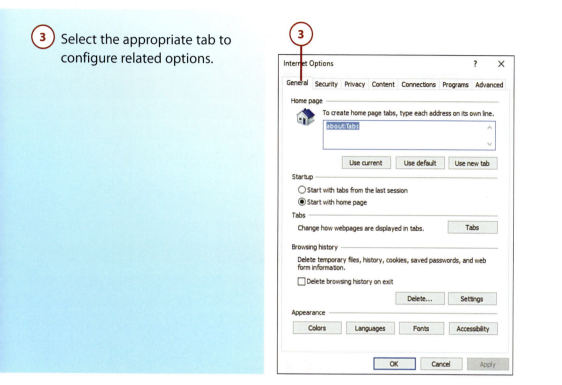

Using Google Chrome

While Edge and Internet Explorer have their fans, the most popular web browser today is Google Chrome. Chrome is a fast and modern browser that works well with Google's various sites and services. It's available for both Windows and Mac operating systems, as well as the Chrome OS used by Google's Chromebook computers.

Sync Your Settings and Bookmarks

While you don't need a Google account to use Chrome, if you sign in to Chrome with your Google account all your personal bookmarks and settings appear, no matter what computer or mobile device you're using.

Open and Browse Web Pages

Google Chrome's interface features many of the same elements found in Microsoft Edge. You enter web addresses into what Google calls the *Omnibox*—Chrome's version of the Address box found in other browsers.

(1) Begin typing the web page address into the Omnibox.

(2) As you type, Google suggests both possible queries and web pages you are likely to visit. Select the page you want from the drop-down list or finish typing the address. Google Chrome now navigates to and displays the page you entered.

(3) To return to the previously viewed page, click the Back button. To move forward again, click the Forward button.

(4) To refresh the current web page, click the Reload This Page button to the left of the Omnibox.

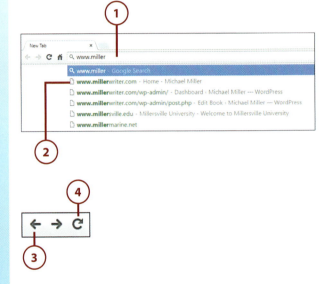

>>>Go Further

LARGER TYPE

Just as you can with Microsoft Edge and Internet Explorer, Chrome lets you zoom in to (or out of) a web page to make the text larger and easier to read. Click the Customize and Control (three bar) button at the top-right corner of the window, go to the Zoom section, and click + to enlarge the page (or click – to make the page smaller).

Work with Tabs

Like Edge and IE, Google Chrome makes good use of tabbed browsing. You can display multiple web pages in multiple tabs, all located in a tab row at the top of the browser window.

① To open a new tab, click the small partial tab at the far right of the row of open tabs. Alternatively, you can click the Customize and Control (three bars) button at the top right and select New Tab, or just press Ctrl+T on your computer keyboard. The new tab opens to the right of the currently open tabs.

Open a Link in a New Tab

You can open any link on a web page in a new tab by right-clicking the link and selecting Open Link as a New Tab.

② To switch to a different tab, click it.

③ To close a tab, click the X on that tab.

Bookmark Favorite Pages

In Google Chrome you keep track of your favorite web pages via the use of *bookmarks*. It's easy to create a bookmark for any web page you're viewing.

(1) Navigate to a given web page and then click the Bookmark This page (star) icon in the Omnibox.

(2) Chrome now displays the Bookmark dialog box. Edit the name of the bookmark if you want.

(3) Bookmarks can be organized in folders. Pull down the Folder list to determine where you want to save this bookmark.

(4) Click the Done button to save the bookmark.

Bookmark

Name: AARP - Health, Travel Deals, Baby Boomers,

Folder: Bookmarks bar

Remove   Edit...   **Done**

Return to a Bookmarked Page

Returning to a bookmarked page is as easy as clicking that bookmark. There are two places you can find bookmarks in Chrome.

1 Click the Customize and Control button and then click Bookmarks. This displays (along with other items) all the bookmarks you've created.

2 Alternatively, display a bookmarks bar beneath the Omnibox by clicking the Customize and Control button, selecting Bookmarks, and then checking Show Bookmarks Bar.

3 Click any bookmark to display that page.

Browse Anonymously in Incognito Mode

If you want or need to keep your browsing private, Google Chrome offers *Incognito mode*, which is similar to Edge's InPrivate browsing. In Incognito mode (actually, a separate browser window), the pages you visit aren't saved to your browser's history file, cookies aren't saved, and your activity is basically done without any record being kept.

(1) Click the Customize and Control button.

(2) Click New Incognito Window.

(3) This opens a new browser window with a little spy icon in the upper-left corner, next to the first tab. When you're done with your private browsing, just close the Incognito window and no one will be the wiser.

Configure Browser Settings

You can configure numerous settings to personalize your Chrome browsing experience.

(1) Click the Customize and Control button.

(2) Click Settings to display a new Settings tab.

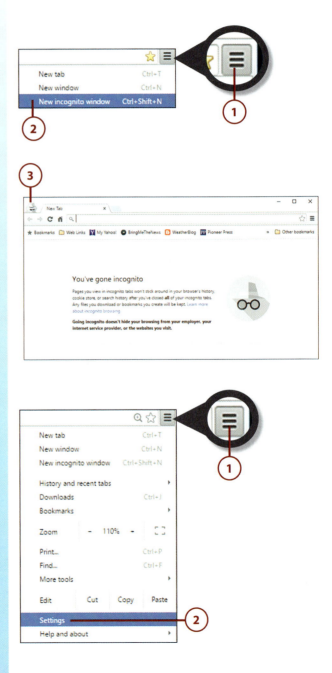

③ Configure any settings as necessary.

③

Chrome	Settings
History	**Sign in**
Extensions	Signed in as molehillgroup@gmail.com. Manage your synced data on Google Dashboard.
Settings	Disconnect your Google Account... Advanced sync settings...
About	**On startup**

On startup

- ● Open the New Tab page
- ○ Continue where you left off
- ○ Open a specific page or set of pages. Set pages

Appearance

Get themes   Reset to default theme

☑ Show Home button
New Tab page Change
☐ Always show the bookmarks bar

Using Mozilla Firefox

Many users swear by Mozilla's Firefox browser. Firefox is a direct descendant of the Netscape browser popular in the early days of the Internet.

Firefox looks and feels a lot like Chrome and Edge. It's a modern browser with tabbed pages and is available for both Windows and Mac operating systems.

Open and Browse Web Pages

Firefox works much like the browsers from Microsoft and Google discussed previously in this chapter. You use Firefox's Address bar to enter the addresses of the web pages you want to visit.

① Begin typing the web page address into the Address bar at the top of the browser window.

② As you type, Firefox suggests web pages you are likely to visit. Select the page you want from the drop-down list or finish typing the address. Firefox now navigates to and displays the page you entered.

①   **②**

Mozilla Firefox Start Page   ✕

www.miller

🔲 Home - Michael Miller
www.millerwriter.com

☐ millerwriter.com
millerwriter.com

3 To return to the previously viewed page, click the Back button. To move forward again, click the Forward button.

4 To refresh the current web page, click the Reload Current Page button on the right side of the Address bar.

>>>Go Further

LARGER TYPE

Just as you can with other browsers, Chrome lets you make the text larger and easier to read. Click the Open Menu (three bar) button at the top-right corner of the window; then click + (Zoom In) to enlarge the page or click – (Zoom Out) to make the page smaller.

Work with Tabs

Firefox was one of the first browsers to make use of tabbed browsing to display multiple web pages in the same window.

1 To open a new tab, click the + at the far right of the row of open tabs. (Alternatively, press Ctrl+T on your computer keyboard.) The new tab opens to the right of the currently open tabs.

2 To switch to a different tab, click it.

3 To change the order of open tabs, click and drag a tab into a new location in the tab row.

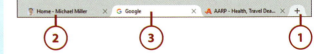

Bookmark Favorite Pages

In Firefox you use bookmarks to keep track of your favorite web pages. It's easy to create a bookmark for any web page you're viewing.

1 Navigate to a given web page and then click the Bookmark This page (star) icon in the toolbar.

Return to a Bookmarked Page

Returning to a bookmarked page is as easy as clicking that bookmark.

1 Click the Show Your Bookmarks button on the toolbar.

2 Click Show All Bookmarks to display the Library window.

3 Select the appropriate folder in the left sidebar.

4 Click any bookmark to return to that page.

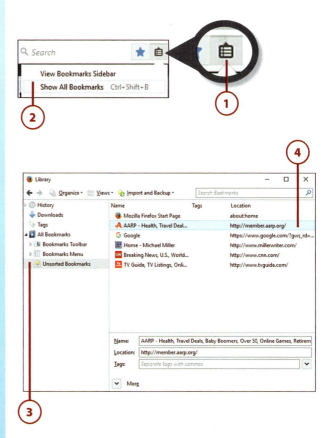

Browse Anonymously in Private Mode

Like the other browsers discussed in this chapter, Firefox offers a Private browsing mode for anonymous (untracked) browsing.

1 Click the Open Menu button.

2 Click New Private Window.

3 This opens a new browser window for private browsing. Close this window when done browsing anonymously.

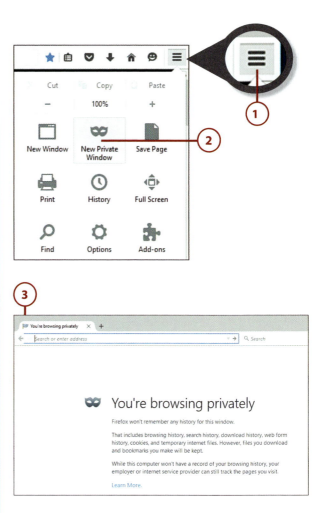

Configure Browser Settings

You can configure numerous settings to personalize your Chrome browsing experience.

1. Click the Open Menu button.

2. Click Options to display a new Preferences page.

3. Configure any settings as necessary.

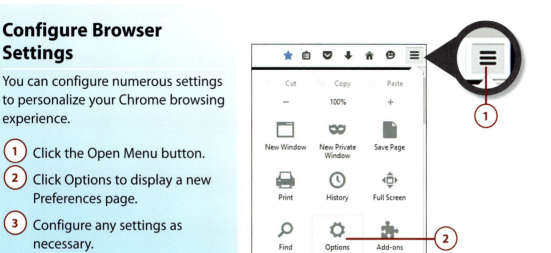

Using Apple Safari

If you have an Apple Macintosh computer, Apple's Safari web browser is built in to the operating system. While you can use other browsers, such as Chrome and Firefox, most Apple users stick with Safari.

Apple Online

Safari is the odd bird of web browsing, in that it's available only for computers running Apple's Mac OS. You can't run Safari on Windows PCs. (There is a version of Safari for Apple's iPhones and iPads, as well—but not for Android devices.)

Open and Browse Web Pages

Safari offers an elegant iTunes-like interface, including tabbed browsing.

1 Position your curser into the Address bar at the top of the browser window and then begin typing the web page address into the Address bar.

2 As you type, Safari suggests web pages you are likely to visit. Select the page you want from the drop-down list or finish typing the address. Safari now navigates to and displays the page you entered.

3 To return to the previously viewed page, click the Back button. To move forward again, click the Forward button.

4 To refresh the current web page, click the Reload Current Page button on the right side of the Address bar.

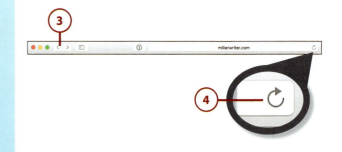

>>>Go Further

LARGER TYPE

You can zoom in to a page in Safari to make the text larger. Press Cmd plus + to zoom in or Cmd plus - to zoom out.

Work with Tabs

Like all other modern web browsers, Safari supports tabbed browsing.

1. To open a new tab, click the + at the right corner of the window, or press Cmd+T. The new tab opens to the right of the currently open tabs.

2. To switch to a different tab, click it.

3. To close a tab, click the X on that tab.

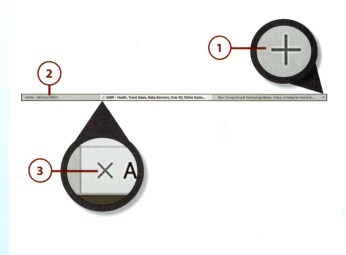

Bookmark Favorite Pages

In Safari you use bookmarks to keep track of your favorite web pages. It's easy to create a bookmark for any web page you're viewing.

1. Navigate to the web page.

2. Click Bookmarks, Add Bookmark (or press Cmd+D).

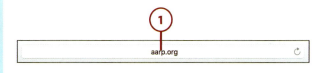

Return to a Bookmarked Page

Returning to a bookmarked page is as easy as clicking that bookmark.

① Click the Sidebar button in the toolbar.

② Click the Bookmarks button.

③ Click the bookmark you want to return to.

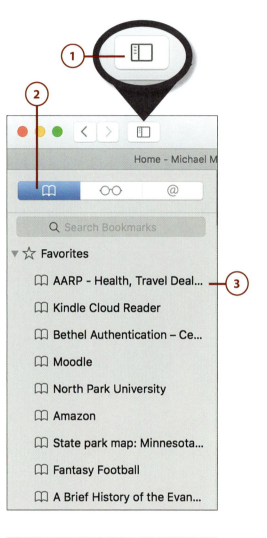

Browse Anonymously in Private Mode

Safari also offers an anonymous browsing mode, dubbed private browsing.

① Click File, New Private Window.

② This opens a new browser window for private browsing; the Address box in this new private menu is black instead of white. Close this window when done browsing anonymously.

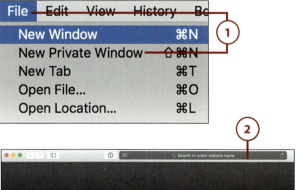

Configure Browser Settings

Like all other browsers, you can configure Safari to your own personal settings.

(1) Click Safari, Preferences to display the Preferences dialog box.

(2) Click a tab and then configure any related settings as necessary.

Bing

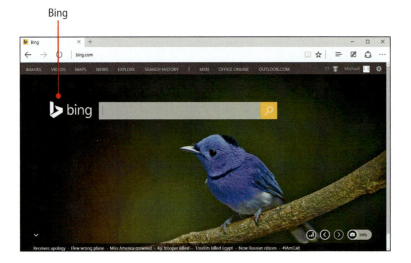

Google

4

Browsing and Searching the Web

Browsing the Web is as easy as entering a URL or clicking a hyperlink on a web page. But how do you find the web pages you want—and the information you need?

How the Web Works

The World Wide Web is the workhorse of the Internet, the place where information of all types is presented in a highly visual format, using a combination of text, images, audio, and even video.

Information on the Web is presented in *web pages*—literally, pages of content on the Web. A web page can contain text, images, video, and links to other web pages. These links are technically known as *hyperlinks*; click a hyperlink and you go to whichever web page it's linked to.

HTML

Web pages are created using a special code, kind of a low-level programming language. This code, called *HTML* (for *HyperText Markup Language*), describes what each element on the web page looks like and how it behaves. Users never see the HTML code; it operates in the background. Instead, you see the result of the code—the web page itself.

Each web page resides at a *website*. A website is nothing more than a collection of web pages residing on a host computer called a *web server*. Servers are constantly connected to the Internet and accessible to all other Internet users.

Every web page has its own unique address, called a *URL*, or *Uniform Resource Locator*. You go to a specific web page by entering its URL into your web browser's Address box, or by clicking a hyperlink to that page from another web page.

Most URLs start with **http://**, add **www.**, continue with the name of the site, and end with **.com**, **.org**, or **.net**. These parts of the URL are identified as follows:

- **Protocol.** This is the **http://** (or, for secure sites, such as shopping sites, **https://**). The protocol identifies the method used to transmit data. For most websites, this is the *HyperText Transfer Protocol* (http).

No http://

You can normally leave off the **http://** when you enter an address into your web browser. In most cases, you can even leave off the **www.** and just start with the domain part of the address.

- **Subdomain.** This is the bit between the // and the first "dot," typically **www.** (As you might expect, the "www" stands for World Wide Web.) Sometimes a subdomain refers to a distinct part of the host website; Microsoft, for example, uses the **windows** subdomain for some of its Windows-related content. (That looks like this: **windows.microsoft.com**).

- **Second-level domain.** This is the part between the two "dots." Most second-level domains identify the company or organization hosting the website. For example, CNN's second-level domain is **cnn**; Walmart's is **walmart**.

- **Top-level domain.** This is the two- or three-letter extension after the final "dot." The top-level domain identifies the type of organization that hosts this website—commercial (**com**), nonprofit organization (**org**), educational organization (**edu**), government (**gov**), and so forth. Different countries have their own top-level domains—**ca** for Canada, **mx** for Mexico, **uk** for the United Kingdom, and so on. And there are all sorts of related domains, such as **net** and **biz** and so forth. But **com** remains the most popular domain for most websites.

Domain Name

Together, the second- and top-level domains comprise the *domain name*. (For example, **site.com** is a domain name.) Each domain name is unique.

The three main parts of a URL (subdomain, second-level domain, and top-level domain) are all separated by "dots." You end up with a complete URL that looks like this: **http://www.site.com**

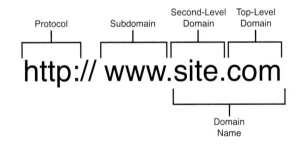

When you enter a site address into your browser, you are automatically taken to the *home page* of that site. The home page often serves as an opening screen that provides a brief overview and a sort of menu of everything you can find at that site.

Home Page

Individual pages on a website have their own unique addresses. Typically, the page name is appended after the domain name, following a backslash (/). For example, if there's a page named **bob** on the **www.site.com** website, that page's full URL would be **www.site.com/bob**.

It's Not All Good

Be Precise

You have to enter web addresses accurately. If you misspell a word or leave out a backslash, it has the same effect as leaving a number out of your street address—it causes your browser to look for the wrong address.

Browsing the Web

Browsing the Web is easy—all you need is a web browser (such as Microsoft Edge or Google Chrome) and some rudimentary navigational skills, and then you're off and running!

Web Browsers

Learn all about web browsers in Chapter 3, "Choosing and Using a Web Browser."

Let's start with the most basic skill, finding and loading a web page. There are two basic ways to go to a web page: Enter the web address manually or click a hyperlink on another web page.

Enter a Web Address

As discussed previously in this chapter, all web pages have their own unique addresses or URLs. To go to a given web page, all you need to know is that page's address.

(**1**) Enter the page's URL into your browser's Address box and press Enter.

(**2**) The browser looks up that page on the Web and starts loading it. When a page is loading, a loading indicator somewhere at the top of your browser (often found in the browser tab or near the Address bar) rotates or flashes or otherwise lets you know that the current task is still in progress. To stop a page before it finishes loading, click the Stop button (actually, the Reload or Refresh button before the page finishes loading) on your browser.

(**3**) The loading indicator stops when all the elements of the page have been downloaded to your computer and displayed in the browser window. To reload the current page, click the Reload or Refresh button.

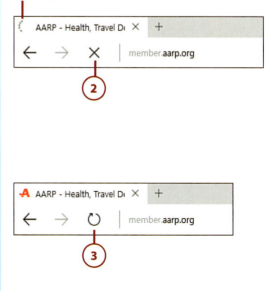

Loading indicator

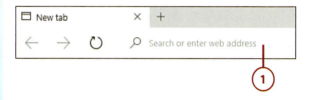

Follow a Link

Most web pages contain hyperlinks (often called just *links*) to other web pages. These links are typically underlined text, although images can also contain links. (Your cursor changes shape, to a pointing hand, when you hover over a link.)

1. To jump to a linked page, click the link on the current web page.

2. Your browser now loads the new page into the current tab. To return to the previous page viewed, click the browser's Back button. (Alternately, you can press the Backspace key on your keyboard.)

Searching the Web

With billions and billions of pages on the Web, finding any given web page (if you don't know its URL) is a daunting challenge. This is why *web search engines*, such as Google and Bing, are consistently among the most popular sites on the Web. You use these search engines to find the websites and pages that you want.

There are several search engines you can use to find things on the Web, including Ask, Bing, Google, and Lycos. The most popular of these is Google, which is used for more than two-thirds of all Web searches; Bing is the only other search provider with double-digit market share. (These are the two search engines featured in this chapter.)

Search Technology

Google and Bing search technologies power several other websites. For example, Google provides search results for AOL's website, and Bing provides search results for Yahoo!.

How Search Engines Work

Google and other search engines scour the billions of pages on the Web to create a virtual snapshot of all those pages. The scouring is accomplished by a special type of software program (called a *spider* or *crawler*). The spider software roams the Web automatically and feeds what it finds back to a massive bank of computers. These computers use this information to create a massive *index* of the Web.

This type of search index is essentially a huge database containing tens of billions of entries. It's important to note that a search index does not contain the original web pages or copies of those pages. The index contains only key information about each page that the spiders find—title, keywords, most important content, and the like—as well as the URLs for each page indexed.

When you conduct a search at Google or Bing, you're not searching the Web, you're searching that particular search index. That is, your query is matched against the information stored in the index database. Pages that best match your query are displayed on a search results page; you click a link in the search results to go to the original page out on the Web.

How Web Searches Work

Every search site on the Web contains two basic components—a search box and a search button. You enter your query—one or more *keywords* that describe what you're looking for—into the search box and then click the search button (or press the Enter key) to start the search.

A typical search takes less than half a second to complete. That's because all the searching takes place on the search engine site's own servers. Remember, when you search Google or Bing, even if you might think you're searching the Web, you're not; you're actually searching that search engine's internal servers. Because you are only searching the limited information stored on these servers, not the entire Web, your searches are completed in the blink of an eye.

The results of your search are displayed on a series of search results pages. Each page typically contains links to and information about 10 or so web pages that match your query, with the best matches listed first. Click the link next to a result to access the matching page.

Constructing an Effective Query

How you construct your search query determines how relevant the results are. The more effective your query, the better targeted the results.

When constructing a query, it's important to focus on the keywords you use because the search sites look for these words when they process your query. Your keywords are compared to the web pages the search site knows about— the more keywords found on a web page, the better the match.

Keywords

Keywords in a query are not case-sensitive; it doesn't matter whether you type **corvette**, **Corvette**, or **CORVETTE**. In addition, it seldom matters in what order you list your keywords. Just make sure to separate each keyword with a space.

You should choose keywords that best describe the information you're looking for, using as many keywords as you need. Don't be afraid of using too many keywords; in fact, using too *few* keywords is a common fault of many novice searchers. The more words you use, the better idea the search engine has of what you're looking for.

For example, if you're looking for information about red 1967 Corvette convertibles, you shouldn't use the single keyword **corvette**. Instead, use all four of the descriptive words to construct the query **red 1967 corvette convertible**. The results will be much more targeted.

>>>Go Further

SEARCHING FOR INFORMATION FOR USERS 50 AND OVER

No doubt you'll use Google or Bing to search for various topics of interest specific to people your age. You want to see results tailored to your age-specific needs, not general results of less interest and value to you.

In some cases, the topic itself defines age-appropriate results. For example, if you search for **retirement communities**, the results you see should link to pages that contain the information for which you're looking.

In other instances, your search query might be more general, and so it will return more general (and less age-specific) results. For example, searching for **Florida vacations** is going to bring up a lot of Mickey Mouse stuff of interest to youngsters and families, but not necessarily the snowbird-related information you were looking for.

In these instances, you can narrow your search results by including the word "seniors" in your query. Even if you don't personally like the term, it's become almost ubiquitous in describing those of us past a certain age, so it's useful as a search term.

So, in the vacation instance, change your query to search for **Florida vacations for seniors** and you'll be much more satisfied with the results. Same thing if you're searching for quilting clubs (**quilting clubs for seniors**), life insurance (**life insurance for seniors**), or comfortable clothing (**comfortable clothing for seniors**); adding a word or two to your main query makes all the difference.

Searching with Google

The number one search engine, in terms of searches and users, is Google (www.google.com). Google is responsible for two-thirds of all the web searches made in the United States, which makes it the default search engine for a majority of Internet users.

Google's popularity is a result of its speed, ease of use, and quality results. Those results, in turn, come from its large search index—and its uncanny capability to match what you're looking for with specific web pages.

More Than Just Search

Google is more than just a simple search engine. You can use Google to display stock quotes (enter the stock ticker), answers to mathematical calculations (enter the equation), and measurement conversions (enter what you want to convert). Google can also track USPS, UPS, and FedEx packages (enter the tracking number), as well as the progress of airline flights (enter the airline and flight number).

Conduct a Basic Search

Initiating a basic search is as easy as entering your query, consisting of one or more keywords, into the search box and then clicking the Google Search button. That's all there is to it—just enter your query, click the Google Search button, and wait for the search results page to display.

1. From within your web browser, enter **www.google.com** into the Address box or Omnibox and then press Enter. This opens Google's main search page.

2. Enter one or more keywords into the Search box.

3. Press Enter or click the Google Search button.

4. When the results are displayed, identify the result you want to view and then click the link for that result. This displays the selected web page within your web browser.

It's Not All Good

Fine-Tune Your Search Results

Google offers a variety of advanced search options to help you fine-tune your search from any search results page.

(1) Conduct a search as normal to display the search results page.

(2) To change the types of results displayed, click one of the links across the top of the page—in this instance, Web (default), Images, Shopping, News, or Videos. (The actual search types displayed depend on your specific query.) Click More to display more types of results— Maps, Books, Flights, and Apps.

(3) Click Search Tools to display filters specific to this type of search.

hamburger bun

Web   Images   Shopping   News   Videos   More ▾   Search tools

4 Click a particular filter to select an option. For example, to display only those results from the past week, click the Time filter (Any Time by default) and then select Past Week. (Available filters differ for different types of search results.)

Advanced Search

Additional search options are found on Google's Advanced Search page, which you get to by clicking the Options (gear) button on any search results page and then selecting Advanced Search. To narrow your search results, all you have to do is make the appropriate selections from the options present.

Search for Images

If you're looking for pictures or illustrations, Google can help with that, too. Click the Images link at the top of any search results page to view only image search results. You can also search directly for images from the Google Image Search site (images.google.com).

1 From within your web browser, enter **images.google.com** into the Address box or Omnibox and then press Enter. This opens Google's Image Search page.

2 Enter one or more keywords that describe the type of image you want into the Search box.

3 Press Enter or click the Google Search button.

4 Click Search Tools at the top of the page to filter your results by image size, color, type, time, usage rights, and so forth.

5 Click an image to display information about that and similar images in a new overlay pane.

6 Click Visit Page to go to the page that hosts this image.

7 Click View Image to display this image only at its original size.

8 Click the X to close the overlay pane and view the rest of the image search results.

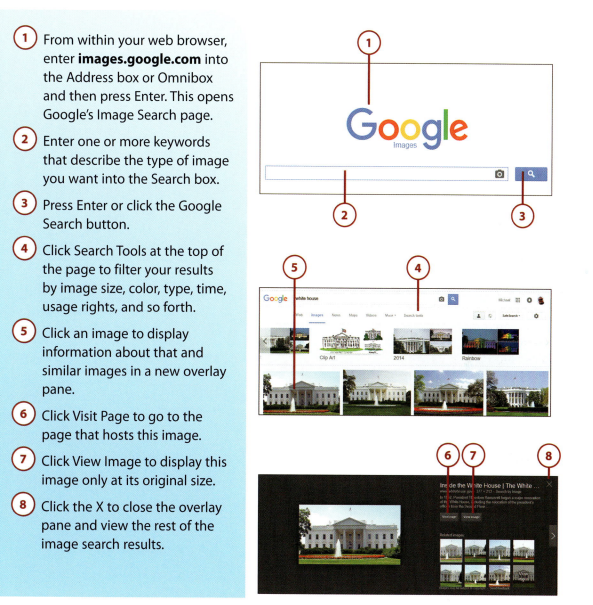

Searching with Bing

Microsoft offers its own search engine that competes with Google. Microsoft's search engine is called Bing (www.bing.com), and it works pretty much like its competitor.

Conduct a Basic Search

① From within your web browser, enter **www.bing.com** into the Address box or Omnibox and press Enter. This opens Bing's main search page.

② Enter one or more keywords into the Search box.

③ Press Enter or click the Search (magnifying glass) button.

④ When the results are displayed, click any page link to view that page.

Fine-Tune Your Search

Bing, like Google, lets you fine-tune your searches in various ways.

① Conduct a search as normal to display the search results page.

② To change the types of results displayed, click one of the links across the top of the page— Web (default), Images, Videos, Maps, or News.

③ Some types of searches offer filters along the top of the search results page. For example, a default web search lets you filter results by when they were posted. (Any Time is the default.) Click a filter to filter the results.

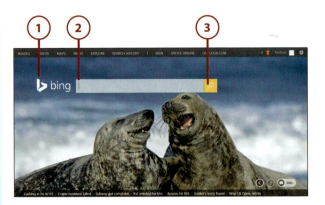

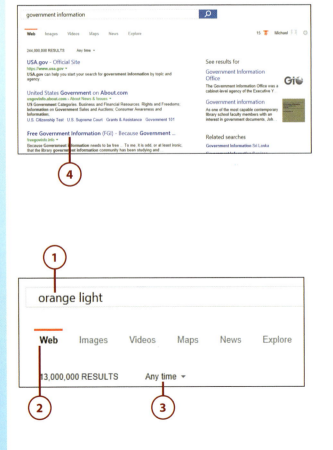

Search for Images

Just as Google offers a discrete image search, so does Bing. It's called Bing Images, and you can find it at www.bing.com/images. (You can also just click Images at the top of any Bing search results page.)

1. From within your web browser, enter **www.bing.com/images** into the Address box or Omnibox and then press Enter. This opens the Bing Images page.

2. Enter one or more keywords that describe the type of image you want into the Search box.

3. Press Enter or click the Search button.

4. Click Search Tools at the top of the page to filter your results by image size, color, type, layout, people, date, and license.

5. Click an image to display information about that and similar images in a new overlay pane.

6. Click View Page to go to the page that hosts this image.

7. Click the picture to display this image only in a new tab.

8. Click the X to close the overlay pane and view the rest of the image search results.

Researching Online with Wikipedia

When you use Google or Bing to search the Web, you're getting unfiltered information from a variety of websites. If you prefer more concise and edited information, check out Wikipedia (www.wikipedia.org).

Wikipedia is like a giant online encyclopedia—but with a twist. Unlike a traditional encyclopedia, Wikipedia's content is created solely by the site's users, resulting in the world's largest online collaboration.

At present, Wikipedia hosts more than 4 million English-language articles, with at least that many articles available in more than 250 different languages. The articles are written and revised by tens of thousands of individual contributors. These users volunteer their time and knowledge at no charge, for the good of the Wikipedia project.

Search Wikipedia

Information on the Wikipedia site is compiled into a series of articles. You search Wikipedia to find the exact articles you need.

1 From within your web browser, enter **www.wikipedia.org** into the Address box or Omnibox and then press Enter. This opens the main Wikipedia page.

2 Enter one or more keywords that describe your search into the Search box; then press Enter.

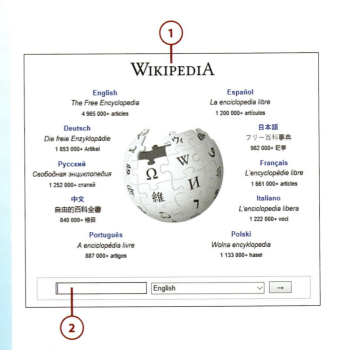

3 If an article directly matches your query, Wikipedia now displays that article. If a number of articles might match your query, Wikipedia displays the list of articles, organized by type or topic. Click the article name to display the specific article.

Read an Article

Each Wikipedia article is organized into a summary and subsidiary sections. Longer articles have a table of contents located beneath the summary. Key information is sometimes presented in a sidebar at the top right of the article.

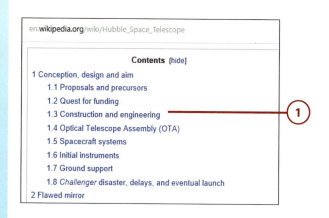

1 Click a link in the Contents box to go directly to that section of the article.

2 Click any link within the body of the article to go to that other article in Wikipedia.

3 Click any footnote number in the body text to go to that footnote at the bottom of the article.

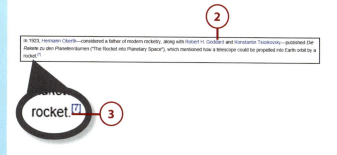

4 Click the footnote link to go to the content referenced elsewhere on the Web.

References [edit]

1. ^ "Fact Sheet" ⟳. *SpaceTelescope.org*. Retrieved October 22, 2013.
2. ^ Ryba, Jeanne. "STS-31" ⟳. NASA. Retrieved March 7, 2012.
3. ^ *a b c d* Harwood, William (May 30, 2013). "Four years after final service call, Hubble Space Telescope going strong" ⟳. *CBS News*. Retrieved June 3, 2013.
4. ^ *a b c d e f g* "HST Satellite details 1990-037B NORAD 20580" ⟳. N2YO. January 27, 2015. Retrieved January 27, 2015.
5. ^ Laidler, Vicki; Bushouse, Howard; Simon, Bernie; Bazell, David (2005). *Synphot User's Guide* 📄 (PDF). Version 5.00. Baltimore, MD: Space Telescope Science Institute. p. 27. Retrieved November 3, 2012.
6. ^ Canright, Shelley. "NASA's Great Observatories" ⟳. NASA. Retrieved April 26, 2008.
7. ^ Oberth, Hermann (1923). *Die Rakete zu den Planetenräumen*. R. Oldenbourg-Verlay. p. 85.

4

It's Not All Good

How Accurate Is Wikipedia?

If anyone can write or edit a Wikipedia article, how are you to know whether the information he or she submits is accurate? While the Wikipedia community is self-policing (and the information generally accurate), misleading or just plain wrong information can seep into the site. It is possible for mistakes to creep into Wikipedia's content and not be discovered by the base of contributing users—and for those mistakes to be reflected in papers and reports written with Wikipedia as the sole source.

It is best, then, to view Wikipedia content as a starting point rather than the final word. When you're writing a scholarly or professional paper, you should not use Wikipedia as your sole source but rather as a guide to additional sources. In addition, it's always a good idea to check the footnotes and other references in a Wikipedia article to confirm the source of information presented; the most accurate articles are well sourced.

Amazon

Lands' End

Staples

Walmart

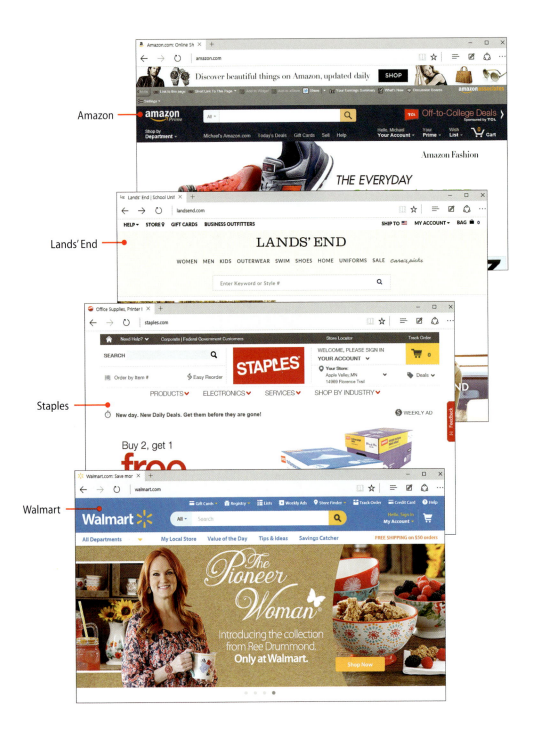

In this chapter, you discover how and where to shop online.

→ Making a Purchase Online

→ How to Shop Safely Online

→ Buying and Selling on eBay

→ Buying and Selling on Craigslist

Shopping Safely Online

One of the most popular uses of the Internet for users of all ages is online shopping. Shopping online is especially practical for shoppers for whom real-world shopping can be inconvenient, at best. Let's face it, it's a lot easier to shop from your computer or tablet screen than it is to drive to and traipse through the local mall.

These days, online shopping is a viable alternative to shopping at brick-and-mortar stores. Almost every major retailer today has an online storefront, offering a similar, if not expanded, selection to what you find on their physical store shelves. And there are plenty of bargains to be had online, too—if you know where to look.

Making a Purchase Online

If you've never shopped online before, you're probably wondering just what to expect. Shopping over the Internet is actually easy; all you need is your computer and a credit card—and an Internet connection, of course.

The online shopping experience is similar from retailer to retailer. You typically go through a multiple-step process that proceeds from discovery to ordering to checkout and payment. We examine each of these steps separately.

Discover Online Retailers

The first step in online shopping is finding where you want to shop. Most major retailers, such as Home Depot (www.homedepot.com), Macy's (www.macys.com), Michaels (www.michaels.com), Staples (www.staples.com), Target (www.target.com), and Walmart (www.walmart.com), have their own websites you can use to shop online. Most catalog merchants, such as Chadwicks of Boston (www.chadwicks.com), Coldwater Creek (www.coldwatercreek.com), Lands' End (www.landsend.com), and L.L.Bean (www.llbean.com), also have their own websites for online ordering.

In addition, many online-only retailers offer a variety of merchandise. These are companies without physical stores; they conduct all their business online and then ship merchandise directly to buyers. These range from smaller niche retailers to larger full-service sites, such as Amazon.com (www.amazon.com) and Overstock.com (www.overstock.com).

In short, you should find no shortage of places to shop online. If worse comes to worst, you can use Google or Bing to search for merchants that sell the specific items in which you're interested.

Search or Browse for Merchandise

| HOME | BED & BATH | WOMEN | MEN | JUNIORS | KIDS | ACTIVE | BEAUTY | SHOES | HANDBAGS | JEWELRY | WATCHES |

Bedding
Bedding Collections
Bed in a Bag
Comforter Sets
Decorative Pillows
Duvet Covers
Quilts & Bedspreads
Sheets
College Lifestyle
Kids' Bedding
Teen Bedding

Bedding Basics
All Bedding Basics
Blankets & Throws

Bath
Bath Robes
Bath Rugs & Bath Mats
Bathroom Accessories
Bath Towels
Beach Towels
Hair Care
Kids' Bath
Personal Care
Shower Curtains & Accessories

Sleep Solutions
Allergy/Asthma Relief
Cool Touch Technology
Heated Bedding

Home Essentials
Dining & Entertaining
Furniture
Kitchen
Luggage
Mattresses
Rugs

More for the Home
Cleaning & Organizing
Cookware
Coffee, Tea & Espresso
Dinnerware
Home Decor
Lighting & Lamps

Brands
Calvin Klein
Charter Club
Croscill
Hotel Collection
INC International Concepts
Lacoste
Martha Stewart Collection
Ralph Lauren
Tommy Hilfiger
Waterford

Bedroom & Mattresses
Beds & Headboards
Kids Furniture

After you've determined where to shop, you need to browse through different product categories on that site or use the site's search feature to find a specific product.

Browsing product categories online is similar to browsing through the departments of a retail store. You typically click a link to access a major product category and then click further links to view subcategories within the main category. For example, the main category might be Clothing; the subcategories might be Men's, Women's, and Children's clothing. If you click the Men's link, you might see a list of further subcategories: Outerwear, Shirts, Pants, and the like. Just keep clicking until you reach the type of item that you're looking for.

Searching for products is often a faster way to find what you're looking for if you have something specific in mind. For example, if you're looking for a women's leather jacket, you can enter the words **women's leather jacket** into the site's search box and get a list of specific items that match those criteria.

The only problem with searching is that you might not know exactly what it is you're looking for; if this describes your situation, you're probably better off browsing. But if you *do* know what you want—and you don't want to deal with lots of irrelevant items—then searching is the faster option.

Examine the Product

Whether you browse or search, you'll probably end up looking at a list of different products on a web page. These listings typically feature one-line descriptions of each item—in most cases, not nearly enough information for you to make an informed purchase.

The thing to do now is to click the link for the item you're particularly interested in. This should display a dedicated product page, complete with a picture and full description of the item. This is where you can read more about the item you selected. Some product pages include different views of the item, pictures of the item in different colors, links to additional information, and maybe even a list of optional accessories that go along with the item. Many sites also offer customer reviews of their products—although you'll need to sort the more useful reviews from the rest.

If you like what you see, you can proceed to the ordering stage. If you want to look at other items, just click your browser's Back button to return to the larger product listing.

Make a Purchase

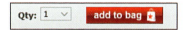

Somewhere on each product description page should be a button labeled Purchase, Buy Now, Add to Cart, Add to Bag, or something similar. This is how you make the actual purchase: by clicking that "buy" button. You don't order the product just by looking at the product description; you have to manually click the "buy" button to place your order.

When you click the "buy" button, that particular item is added to your *shopping cart*. That's right, the online retailer provides you with a virtual shopping cart that functions just like a real-world shopping cart. Each item you choose to purchase is added to your virtual shopping cart.

In-stock Notification

The better online retailers tell you either on the product description page or during the checkout process whether an item is in stock. Look for this information to help you decide how to group your items for shipment.

After you've ordered a product and placed it in your shopping cart, you can choose to shop for other products on that site or proceed to the site's checkout. It's important to note that when you place an item in your shopping cart, you haven't actually completed the purchase yet. You can keep shopping (and adding more items to your shopping cart) as long as you want.

You can even decide to abandon your shopping cart and not purchase anything at this time. All you have to do is leave the website, and you won't be charged for anything. It's the equivalent of leaving your shopping cart at a real-world retailer and walking out the front door; you don't actually buy anything until you walk through the checkout line. (Although, with some sites, the items remain in your shopping cart—so they'll be there waiting for you the next time you shop!)

Check Out and Pay

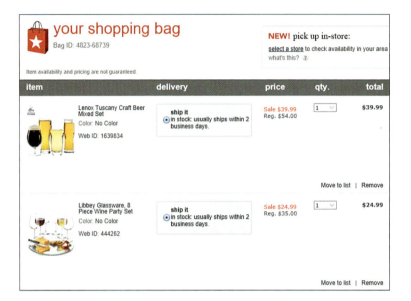

To finalize your purchase, you have to visit the store's *checkout*. This is like the checkout line at a traditional retail store; you take your virtual shopping cart through the checkout, get your purchases totaled, and then pay for what you're buying.

The checkout at an online retailer typically consists of one or more web pages with forms you have to fill out. If you've visited the retailer before, the site might remember some of your personal information from your previous visit. Otherwise, you have to enter your name, address, and phone number, as well as the address you want to ship the merchandise to (if that's different from your billing address). You also have to pay for the merchandise, typically by entering a credit card number.

The checkout provides one last opportunity for you to change your order. You can delete items you decide not to buy or change quantities on any item. At some merchants you can even opt to have your items gift-wrapped and sent to someone as a present. You should be able to find all these options somewhere in the checkout process.

You might also have the option of selecting different types of shipping for your order. Many merchants offer both regular and expedited shipping—the latter for an additional charge.

Another option at some retailers is to group all items for reduced shipping cost. (The alternative is to ship items individually as they become available.) Grouping items is attractive cost-wise, but you can get burned if one of the items is out of stock or not yet available; you could end up waiting weeks or months for those items that could have been shipped immediately.

After you've entered all the appropriate information, you're asked to place your order. This typically means clicking a button that says Place Your Order or something similar. You might even see a second screen asking you whether you *really* want to place your order, just in case you have second thoughts.

After you place your order, you see a confirmation screen, typically displaying your order number. Write down this number or print this page; you need to refer to this number if you have to contact customer service. Most online merchants also send you a confirmation message, including this same information, via email.

That's all there is to it. You shop, examine the product, place an order, proceed to checkout, and pay. It's that easy!

>>>Go Further
FINDING THE BEST BARGAINS ONLINE

If you have no preference as to which online retailers to shop, you can use a *price comparison site* to help find the best merchandise and pricing online. These sites let you search for specific products and then sort and filter the results in a number of different ways.

Some of the most popular price comparison sites include the following:

- BizRate (www.bizrate.com)
- Google Shopping (www.google.com/shopping)
- mySimon (www.mysimon.com)
- NexTag (www.nextag.com)

- PriceGrabber (www.pricegrabber.com)
- Shopping.com (www.shopping.com)
- Yahoo! Shopping (shopping.yahoo.com)

Many of these price comparison sites include customer reviews of both the products and the available merchants. Some even let you perform side-by-side comparisons of multiple products, which is great if you haven't yet made up your mind as to what you want to buy.

How to Shop Safely Online

Shopping online is every bit as safe as shopping at your local retail store. The big online retailers are just as reputable as traditional retailers, offering safe payment, fast shipping, and responsive service.

Shop Safely

Some consumers are wary about buying items online, but online shopping can be as safe as shopping at a traditional brick-and-mortar retailer—as long as you take the proper precautions.

1 Make sure the online retailer prominently displays its contact information and offers multiple ways to connect. You want to be able to call the retailer if something goes wrong—and not rely solely on email communication.

2 Look for the site's return policy and satisfaction guarantee. You want to be assured that you'll be taken care of if you don't like what you ordered.

3 A reputable site should tell you whether an item is in stock and how long it will take to ship— before you place your order.

4 For the best protection, pay by major credit card. Many retailers also let you use PayPal to pay via credit or debit card, or electronic funds transfer from your bank.

5 Make sure the retailer uses a secure server for its checkout process. Look in the Address box for the letters **https://** (not the normal http://) before the URL; you should also see the "lock" symbol before or after the address. If the checkout process is not secure, do not proceed with payment.

Returns or Exchanges by Mail in Two Easy Steps

1. **Complete a Return and Exchange Form**

Download and complete the online form, or use the form printed on the packing slip that came with your order.

▸ **Print a Return and Exchange Form** (PDF)

2. **Print a Prepaid Return Label**

Please note: **L.L.Bean Visa Cardmembers receive free returns** when using our prepaid return labels: **for all others, your refund will be reduced by $6.50.**

▸ **Prepaid label for US or Puerto Rico** (opens in a new window)
Ship your return via UPS (our preferred method) or US Postal Service.

▸ Prepaid label for APO/FPO or US Territories (PDF)
Returns from these locations must be sent via US Postal Service.

Samsung UN19F4000
19" 720p LED-LCD HDTV
Item #: 30519F4000

✔ In Stock

Accepted forms of payment:

🔒 Target Brands Inc [US] | https://www-secure.target.com/c

>>>*Go Further*

CREDIT CARD PROTECTIONS

Believe it or not, the safest way to shop online is to pay via credit card. That's because credit card purchases are protected by federal law—and, in many cases, by the card issuer.

Under federal law you have the right to dispute certain charges, and your liability for unauthorized transactions is limited to $50. In addition, some card issuers offer a supplemental guarantee that says you're not responsible for *any* unauthorized charges made online. Of course, you should read your card's statement of terms to determine the company's exact liability policy.

Buying and Selling on eBay

Some of the best bargains on the Internet come from other consumers, just like you, selling their own items online. The most popular website for individual sales is eBay (www.ebay.com), which is an online marketplace that facilitates transactions between people and businesses that have things to sell and customers who want to buy those things.

The sellers on eBay can opt to sell their products via traditional fixed-priced transactions or via *online auctions*. An online auction is, quite simply, a web-based version of a traditional auction. You find an item you want to own and then place a bid on it. Other users also place bids, and at the end of the auction—typically a seven-day period—the highest bidder wins.

Professional Sellers

Not all eBay sellers are individuals. There are many professional sellers on eBay, as well as traditional retailers selling either via online auction or at a fixed price.

Bid in an eBay Auction

Many (but not all) of the items for sale on eBay are offered via the online auction process. In an online auction, interested shoppers place bids on a given item; the person who places the highest bid wins the auction and gets to purchase the item.

An eBay auction is kind of like a traditional auction—you know, the type where a fast-talking auctioneer stands in the front of the room, trying to coax potential buyers into bidding *just a little bit more* for the piece of merchandise up for bid. The only difference is that there's no fast-talking auctioneer online (the bidding process is executed by special auction software on the eBay site), and your fellow bidders aren't in the same room with you—in fact, they might be located anywhere in the world. Anyone who has Internet access and is registered with eBay can be a bidder.

---

eBay Account

There is no cost to register with eBay, although if you want to sell items, you have to provide your credit card and checking account numbers. (eBay uses this information to help weed out potential scammers and to provide a billing option for the seller's eBay fees.)

The bidding process itself is automated; you don't have to keep entering higher and higher bids as other bidders enter the auction. All you have to do is enter the maximum amount you're willing to pay. eBay's bidding software automatically places a bid for you that bests the current bid by a specified amount—but doesn't reveal your maximum bid.

For example, the current bid on an item might be $25. You're willing to pay up to $40 for the item and enter a maximum bid of $40. eBay's "proxy" software places a bid for you in the amount of $26—higher than the current bid, but less than the specified maximum bid.

If there are no other bids, you'll win the auction with a $26 bid. Other potential buyers, however, can place additional bids; unless their maximum bids are more than the current bidder's $40 maximum, they are informed (by email) that they have been outbid—and your current bid is automatically raised to match the new bids (up to the specified maximum bid price).

So, depending on what other bidders do, you may end up winning the auction for less than your maximum bid. You may win with your maximum bid. Or you may lose (and therefore not get to purchase the item) if someone outbids you.

(1) From the eBay home page, search or browse for an item you want.

(2) Click the item you want to purchase. This displays the item's product page.

(3) If the item is offered via auction, you see a Bid section with either the starting bid or current bid displayed. Enter the maximum amount you're willing to pay into the bid box; then click Place Bid. (Your bid amount has to be equal to or greater than the seller's starting bid, or higher than any other existing bids.)

4 At this point, eBay's built-in bidding software automatically places a bid for you. You are notified if your bid is the current high bid or if you've already been outbid by another bidder. If you have been outbid, you can place another bid at a higher price. If you're the high bidder, sit tight.

5 At the conclusion of an auction, eBay informs you if you're the high bidder. You are then prompted to pay for the item (typically via the PayPal service), and the seller ships it to you.

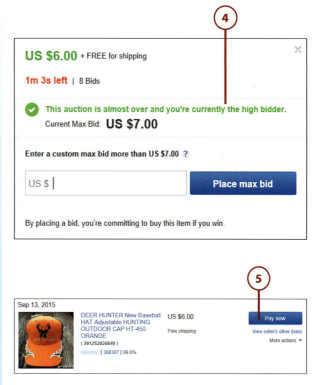

My eBay

You can monitor the progress of all your current eBay activity from the My eBay page. Just click the My eBay link at the top of eBay's home page.

Buy a Fixed Price Item

Not all items on eBay are offered via auction. Many items are sold in a more conventional fashion, at a fixed price.

Fixed-price items are offered on eBay via what it calls the Buy It Now option. In some instances, Buy It Now is the only option offered; you click the button and purchase the item at the stated price. Other items are offered for auction with a Buy It Now option; you can place a bid and hope you win at a lower price, or just click the Buy It Now button to purchase the item now at a higher price.

1 From the eBay home page, search or browse for an item you want.

2 Click the item you want to purchase. This displays the item's product page.

3 If the item is offered at a fixed price, you see the item's price and a Buy It Now button. Click the Buy It Now button.

4 You are now prompted to pay for the item. Follow the onscreen instructions to make payment, typically via PayPal.

It's Not All Good

Protecting Yourself Against Fraudulent Sellers

When you're bidding for and buying items on eBay, you're pretty much in "buyer beware" territory. You agree to buy an item, almost sight unseen, from someone whom you know practically nothing about. You pay for the item and hope and pray that you get something shipped back in return—and that the thing shipped is the thing you thought you were buying in good condition. If you don't like what you get—or if you receive nothing at all—the seller has your money. And what recourse do you have?

The first line of defense against frauds and cheats is to intelligently choose the people you deal with. On eBay, the best way to do this is via the Feedback system. Next to every seller's name is a number and percentage, which represents that seller's Feedback rating. You should always check a seller's Feedback rating before you bid. If the number is high with an overwhelmingly positive percentage, you can feel safer than if the seller has a lot of negative feedback. For even better protection, click the seller's name in the item listing to view his Member Profile, where you can read individual feedback comments. Be smart and avoid those sellers who have a history of delivering less than what was promised.

What do you do if you follow all this advice and still end up receiving unacceptable merchandise—or no merchandise at all? Fortunately, eBay offers a Money Back Guarantee for any transaction gone bad. Just go to eBay's Resolution Center (resolutioncenter.ebay.com) and follow the onscreen instructions to notify eBay of the issue and get it taken care of.

Sell an Item

Have some old stuff in your garage or attic that you want to get rid of? Consider selling it on eBay. Selling on eBay is a little more involved than bidding but can generate big bucks if you do it right.

Before you list your first item, however, you need to do a little homework. That means determining what you're going to sell and for how much, as well as how you're going to describe the item. You need to write a full item description, as well as take a few digital photos of the item to include with the listing.

When the auction is over or the item is sold at a fixed price, eBay notifies you (via email) and provides the email address of the winning bidder. Most buyers pay via credit card (using the PayPal service). Once you receive notice of payment, pack the item and ship it out.

eBay Fees

eBay makes its money by charging sellers two types of fees. (Buyers don't pay fees to eBay.) *Insertion fees* are based on the minimum bid or reserve price of the item listed. *Final value fees* are charged when you sell an item, based on the item's final selling price. Fees are typically charged directly to the seller's credit card account.

(1) Click the Sell link on eBay's home page.

(2) Enter the title for your item listing; then click the Get Started button. (If the item has a UPC or ISBN, you can enter that number instead of a title; eBay then displays information specific to that item.)

(3) Select the appropriate category for your item; then click the Create Listing button.

(4) On the next page, in the Describe Your Item section, fill in or select the requested information. You should also upload at least one photo of the item you're selling.

Daily Deals | Gift Cards | Sell

Sell

1

Tell us what you're selling

Give us a title for your listing (include brand, size, color, material, etc.)

Get started

E.g.: Men's blue adidas Glide running shoes size 11 | You can also enter the UPC, ISBN, or part number of your item

2

Select a matching category for your item:

○ Clothing, Shoes & Accessories > Women's Accessories > Gloves & Mittens
◉ Clothing, Shoes & Accessories > Men's Accessories > Gloves & Mittens
○ Sporting Goods > Cycling > Cycling Clothing > Gloves

Select another category

Create listing

3

4

Describe your item

* Title   Gloves

* Condition   -

* Photos   Add up to 12 photos for free.
                 Add photos

Item specifics   ☐ Add item specifics (recommended)

* Details   Times New Roman ∨   10 ∨   B   I   U   ☰   Switch to HTML editor

5 Scroll to the Select Format and Price section and then click either Auction or Fixed Price. When prompted, enter the starting bid or fixed price of the item.

6 Scroll to the How You'll Ship It section and enter the requested information about how you'll ship the item, and how much you'll charge for shipping.

7 Click the List It button to complete your listing and take it live.

5

Select format and price

* Listing format	Auction is best when you're not sure how much your item could sell for.	Fixed price is best when you know how much you want to get.
	Auction	**Fixed price**

* Starting price $

Tip: Consider setting the starting price at the minimum you're comfortable with. Your item won't sell for less than this amount.

☐ Add Buy It Now ⓘ

☐ Add a reserve price (fee varies) ⓘ
Tip: Most items sell best without a reserve price. Rather than add a reserve price, consider increasing your starting price or switching to a fixed price format.

* Listing duration   7 days   ▾

6

How you'll ship it

Select shipping for me   Select shipping myself   Offer local pickup only

We'll apply this option based on how similar items shipped. Learn more

USPS First Class Package (2 to 6 business days) — Package (or thick envelope) — 4oz. — 7.0in. x 4.0in. x 4.0in.
Estimated shipping cost: **$2.74**
☐ Offer free shipping

7

>>>*Go Further*

PAYPAL

PayPal is a payment service, previously owned by eBay, that facilitates online payments for eBay and various online retailers. As a shopper, you open a PayPal account and provide information about how you want to pay for things—via credit card, debit card, or debit from your checking account. Then, when you go to pay for an eBay item or check out when shopping at an online merchant, all you have to do is log in to your PayPal account (from eBay or the merchant's site) and all your payment and shipping information is entered automatically. (If you don't yet have a PayPal account, you can create one at www.paypal.com.)

Some people find paying via PayPal is quicker and easier than entering a credit card at each site you use; others use PayPal only to pay for eBay items (where it's pretty much required).

Buying and Selling on Craigslist

When you're looking to buy something locally, you can often find great bargains on Craigslist (www.craigslist.org), an online classified advertising site. Browse the ads until you find what you want and then arrange with the seller to make the purchase.

Other Services

The Craigslist site isn't just for buying and selling merchandise. You can also use Craigslist to look for or offer services, jobs, and housing.

Buy an Item on Craigslist

Listings on Craigslist are just like traditional newspaper classified ads. All transactions are between you and the seller; Craigslist is just the "middleman." That means when you purchase an item from a Craigslist seller, expect to pick up the item in person and pay in cash.

1. From the Craigslist home page (www.craigslist.org), click US to see a list of states and cities with Craigslist listings and then click the name of your city.

2. Go to the For Sale section and click the category you're looking for.

3. Click the link or picture for the item you're interested in.

4. Read the item details; then click the Reply button to email the seller and express your interest.

Contacting the Seller

When you contact the seller via email, let him know you're interested in the item and want to see it in person. The seller should reply with a suggested time and place to view and possibly purchase the item.

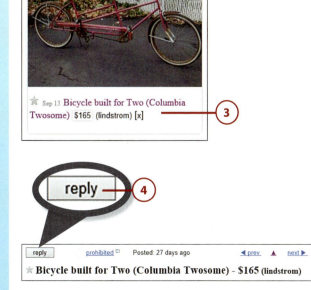

It's Not All Good

Buyer Beware

Just as with traditional classified ads, Craigslist offers no buyer protections. You're typically paying cash, and you're out the money if the item isn't what you were looking for. For that reason, you need to fully inspect items before purchasing. In addition, you might want to take someone with you when picking up an item at the buyer's house or apartment—or agree to meet at a neutral location, instead.

Sell an Item on Craigslist

The Craigslist site is also a great place to sell items you want to get rid of. Just place an ad and wait for potential buyers to contact you!

1. From the Craigslist site, click the Post to Classifieds link.

2. Click the type of ad you want to place—typically For Sale by Owner.

3. Click the category that best fits what you're selling. (If necessary, click through to an appropriate subcategory.)

craigslist

post to classifieds — ①
my account

what type of posting is this: (see prohibited list before posting.)

○ job offered
○ gig offered (I'm hiring for a short-term, small or odd job)
○ resume / job wanted

○ housing offered
○ housing wanted

● for sale by owner
○ for sale by dealer
○ wanted by owner
○ wanted by dealer

②

please choose a category: (see prohibited list and recall information before posting.)

○ antiques - by owner
○ appliances - by owner
○ arts & crafts - by owner
○ atvs, utvs, snowmobiles - by owner
○ auto parts - by owner
○ baby & kid stuff - by owner (no illegal sales of recall items, e.g. drop-side cribs, recalled strollers)
○ barter
○ bicycle parts - by owner
○ bicycles - by owner

③

4 Enter the necessary details about you and what you're selling, including the listing title, asking price, and description; then click Continue.

5 You are now prompted to add pictures of your item. (Items sell better if buyers can see what's for sale, although such photos are optional.) Click the Add Images button to select digital photos of your item.

6 Click the Done with Images button.

7 Confirm the listing details and then click the Publish button to finalize the listing.

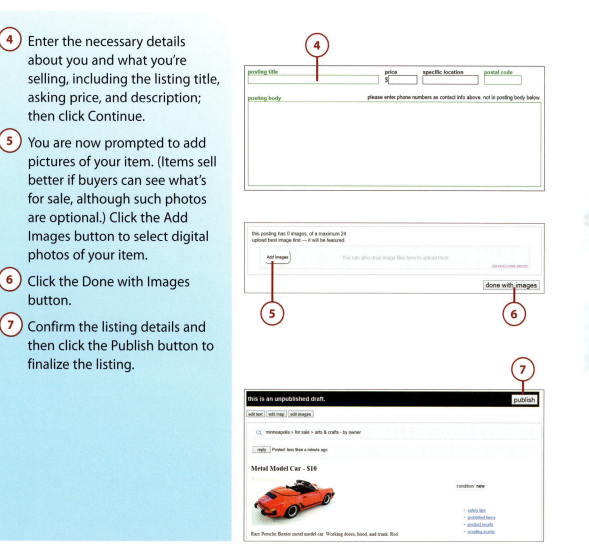

It's Not All Good

Safety First

Make sure someone else is with you before you invite potential buyers into your home to look at the item you have for sale—or if you go to a seller's house to buy something. It's always better to arrange to meet buyers at a safe neutral (and public) location.

>>>*Go Further*
MAKING TRAVEL PLANS ONLINE

The Internet is also a great place to find all sorts of travel bargains from the comfort of your own living room. Whether you're looking for hotels, flights, rental cars, or cruises, you can find and book them all online.

Here's what you can find:

- **Hotels.** You can make hotel reservations directly at the websites of most big hotel chains. Some of the most popular chains include Choice Hotels (www.choicehotels.com for Comfort Inn, Quality Inn, Clarion, and EconoLodge), Hilton (www.hilton.com for Doubletree, Embassy Suites, Hampton Inn, Homewood Suites, and Hilton), Hyatt (www.hyatt.com for Hyatt and Hyatt Place), and Marriott (www.marriott.com for Courtyard, Fairfield Inn and Suites, Marriott, Residence Inn, Springhill Suites, and TownPlace Suites); use your favorite search engine to search for other hotels you like.

- **Airline flights.** You can make flight reservations directly from the websites of major carriers. Some of the most popular airline sites include American Airlines (www.aa.com), Delta (www.delta.com), Southwest (www.southwest.com), and United (www.united.com).

- **Rental cars.** Book rental cars directly from Avis (www.avis.com), Budget (www.budget.com), Enterprise (www.enterprise.com), Hertz (www.hertz.com), and other major car rental companies.

In addition to booking hotel rooms, flights, and rental cars directly, you can also use any of the several general online travel sites to book some or all of your trip needs. These sites let you book hotels, rental cars, flights, cruises—you name it—and include Expedia (www.expedia.com), Orbitz (www.orbitz.com), Travelocity (www.travelocity.com), TripAdvisor (www.tripadvisor.com), and AARP Travel (http://travel.aarp.org). Most of these sites offer discounted rates, specials, and package deals often not available from the major hotel, airline, and rental car sites. You'll also find lots of user reviews, which can be useful when deciding where to go or stay on your next trip.

Facebook

LinkedIn

Pinterest

Twitter

In this chapter, you learn how to connect with friends and family via Facebook and other social media.

→ Using Facebook
→ Using LinkedIn
→ Using Pinterest
→ Using Twitter

Using Facebook and Other Social Media

A social network is a website community that enables users to connect with and share their thoughts, activities, pictures, and even videos with one another. Think of it as an online network of friends and family, including former schoolmates, coworkers, and neighbors.

The most popular social network today is Facebook, with more than 1.5 billion users worldwide. Facebook isn't the only social network popular among users 50 and over, however; you may also be interested in LinkedIn, Pinterest, and Twitter.

Using Facebook

When you want to keep track of what friends and family are up to and keep them up to date on your activities, there's no better place to do it than Facebook. Write one post, and it's seen by hundreds of your online "friends." It's the easiest way I know to connect with almost everyone you know.

Although Facebook started life as a social network for college students, it has since expanded its membership lists and is now the preferred social network for more mature users. (In fact, the fastest growing segment of Facebook users are those aged 45+.)

People of any age can use Facebook to connect with current family members and reconnect with friends from the past. If you want to know what your friends from high school or the old neighborhood have been up to over the past several decades, chances are you can find them on Facebook.

Sign Up and Sign In

To use Facebook, you must sign up for a free account, which you can do at www.facebook.com. Once you have an account, return to Facebook's home page and enter your email address or username and password to sign in.

Discover Friends on Facebook

To connect with someone on Facebook, you must become mutual *friends*. A Facebook friend can be a real friend or a family member, colleague, acquaintance—you name it. When you add someone to your Facebook friends list, he sees everything you post—and you see everything he posts.

The easiest way to find friends on Facebook is to let Facebook find them for you—based on the information you provide for your personal profile. The more Facebook knows about you, especially in terms of where you've worked and gone to school, the more friends it can find.

Friend Requests

Facebook doesn't automatically add a person to your friends list. Instead, that person receives an invitation ("friend request") to be your friend; she can accept or reject the invitation. To accept or reject any friend requests you receive, click the Friend Request button on the Facebook toolbar. (And don't worry; if you reject a request, that person won't be notified.)

1. Log in to your Facebook account and click the Friends button on the Facebook toolbar.

2. The pull-down menu lists any friend requests you've received and offers a number of friend suggestions from Facebook (People You May Know). To add one of these people to your friends list, click the Add Friend button.

Suggested Friends

The people Facebook suggests as friends are typically people who went to the same schools you did, worked at the same companies you did, or are friends of your current friends.

3. To continue searching for friends, click Find Friends at the top of the menu to display your Friends page.

4. To find people in your email contacts list who are also members of Facebook, go to the Add Personal Contacts section at the top of the Friends page. Click the email service you use, enter any requested information (typically your email address and password), and then click the Find Friends button.

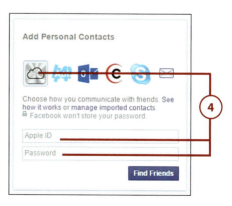

5 Facebook lists all matching contacts. Check the people you want to add as a friend and then click the Add Friends button to send friend requests.

Find Friends

You can also find Facebook friends who come from your hometown, went to your school, or worked at the same company you did. Learn more in Chapter 7, "Finding Old Friends—And Making New Ones."

You have one Outlook.com (Hotmail) contact on Facebook that you can add as your friend.

Select which contacts to add as a friend from the list below. You can also try another email account to find more friends.

Step 1 Find Friends	Step 2 Add Friends	Step 3 Invite Friends

☑ Select All Friends

☑ Sam Spade

Add Friends   Skip

5

Post a Status Update

To let your family and friends know what you've been up to, you need to post what Facebook calls a *status update*. Every status update you make is broadcast to everyone on your friends list, displayed in the News Feed on their home pages. A basic status update is text only, but you can also include photos, videos, and links to other web pages in your posts.

1 Click Home on the Facebook toolbar to return to your home page.

1

2 Type a short message into the Update Status box at the top of the page. As you type, the box expands slightly to offer more options.

3 If you're with someone else and want to mention them in the post, click the Tag People in Your Post button and enter that person's name.

4 If you want to include your current location in your post, click the Add a Location to Post button and enter the city or place you're at.

5 To determine who can read this post, click the Privacy button and make a selection.

Who Sees Your Posts?

You can opt to make any post Public (meaning anyone can read it), visible only to your Friends, visible only to yourself (Only Me), or Custom (you select individuals who can and can't view it).

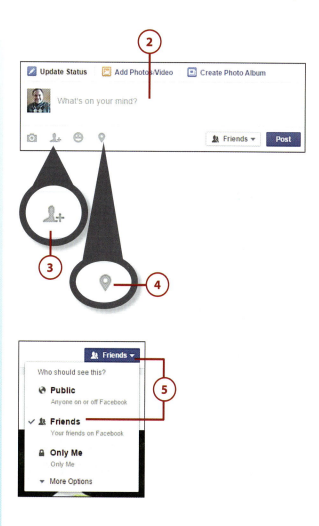

6 To include a link to another web page, enter that page's URL in your status update. Facebook should recognize the link and display an image from that page. Click the forward and back buttons to cycle through and choose which image to display in your post.

7 To include a picture or video with your post, click Add Photos/Video to display the Open dialog box; then select the photos or videos to include.

8 When you're ready to post your update, click the Post button.

>>>Go Further
FACEBOOK PRIVACY

Facebook likes to share all your information with just about everybody on its social network—not just your friends or their friends, but also advertisers and third-party websites. Fortunately, you can configure Facebook to be much less public than it could be, and thus keep your private information private.

The first step to ensuring your Facebook privacy is to determine who, by default, can see all the posts you make. You can do this in a positive fashion, by telling Facebook precisely who can view your new posts. You can also take a more negative (or defensive) approach, by telling Facebook who can't see your status updates. Click the Privacy Shortcuts button on the Facebook toolbar and then click the down arrow next to Who Can See My Stuff? Go to the Who Can See My Future Posts? section, click the down arrow, and select one of the resulting options. Click Public to let anyone on Facebook see your posts; click Friends to restrict viewing to only people on your Facebook friends list; click Only Me to keep your posts totally private—that is, to keep anyone from seeing them; or click More Options to create a custom list of people who can or can't see your posts.

Even after you set these global posting privacy settings, you can change the privacy setting for any individual post you make. That is, any given post can be sent to a specific list of people that overrides the global settings you made previously, and set a new default for future posts. Just click the Post Privacy Setting button when creating a new status update and make a selection from the options there.

Additional privacy settings are available by clicking on the Privacy Shortcuts button on the toolbar. Beyond that, remember to use common sense when posting to Facebook and other social networks. Don't post overly personal information, especially contact information (street address, phone number, and so forth). Don't post anything you wouldn't want your spouse or grandkids or neighbors to see. Avoid posting embarrassing or controversial information or opinions. And always—always!—think twice before posting. Facebook is not your own private diary; it's a public forum where just about everything you post can be read by all other users.

Find Out What Your Friends Are Up To

Your home page on Facebook displays a News Feed of all the status updates made by people on your friends list. The newest posts are at the top; scroll down through the list to read older posts.

1. Click Home on the Facebook toolbar to return to your home page.

2 Your friends' posts are displayed in the News Feed in the middle of the page. To leave your own comments about a post, click Comment and then enter your text into the resulting text box.

3 To "like" a post, click Like.

4 If a post includes a link to another web page, that link appears beneath the post, along with a brief description of the page. Click the link to open the other page in your web browser.

5 If a post includes one or more photos, click the photo to view it in a larger onscreen lightbox.

6 If a post includes a video (which is indicated by a Play icon in the middle of the thumbnail), click the video thumbnail to begin playback.

Explore Your Friends' Timelines

If you want to know what an old friend has been up to over the years, you can find out by visiting that person's Facebook Timeline. As the name implies, this is a "timeline" of that person's posts and major life events. It also displays that person's personal information, photos and videos, upcoming events, and the like.

1 Click a person's name anywhere on the Facebook site to display his or her profile or Timeline page.

Rudolfo Lasperi
1 hr ·

It's spring -- check out this beautiful flower in our garden.

Like Comment Share

5

Lew Archer at Rambling River Park
2015 · Farmington, MN · ⊙ ·

Grandkids on the playground

Like   Comment   Share

6

Lew Archer
13 mins ·

Here's a good looking bird.

1

2 Click About to view key personal information.

3 Click Friends to view a list of this person's friends.

4 Click Photos to view your friend's photos.

5 View a person's status updates in reverse chronological order (newest first) in the right-hand column on the Timeline.

Using LinkedIn

Facebook isn't the only social network of interest to adults 50 and over. LinkedIn is different from Facebook and most other social media in that it has a distinct focus on business. Businesses use LinkedIn to find potential employees; job hunters use LinkedIn to look for potential employers; and business professionals use LinkedIn to keep in touch with former colleagues and others in their professions.

Even if you're not currently in the job market, LinkedIn is a great way to network with other people in your industry and to keep tabs on what former coworkers are up to. It's very much a business networking site, using social networking functionality.

Creating a LinkedIn Account

A basic LinkedIn account is free. (LinkedIn also offers several types of premium accounts, primarily for jobseekers and salespeople seeking leads.) Sign up and create your profile at www.linkedin.com.

Edit Your Profile

Every LinkedIn member has her own personal profile page. This profile page is what other LinkedIn users see when they search for you on the site; it's where you make your initial impression to the people you want to make contact with—including potential employers.

Your LinkedIn profile is kind of like a mini-resume, containing important personal and professional information. It's also fully customizable; you can select which content others see.

1 On the LinkedIn menu bar, click Profile and select Edit Profile. This displays your profile page.

2 The snapshot section at the top of the page contains any information you entered when you signed up for your LinkedIn account. To edit any existing information, mouse over that item and click the Edit (pencil) icon to display the editing pop-up.

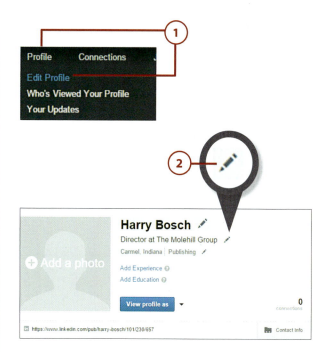

3 Edit the desired information.

4 Click the Save button.

Find New Connections

LinkedIn's equivalent of Facebook friends is called *connections*. These are business or professional contacts whom you know and trust. Anyone on the LinkedIn site can become a connection; you can also invite people who are not yet LinkedIn members to join your connections list. As with Facebook friends, people on LinkedIn have to accept your invitation before they become connections.

To establish new connections, you can search for current LinkedIn members in your email contacts list or invite other email contacts to join LinkedIn.

Find Former Colleagues

LinkedIn also lets you search for people who've worked at the same companies you've worked at. Learn more in Chapter 7.

1 From the LinkedIn menu bar, click Connections and then select Add Connections to display the See Who You Already Know on LinkedIn page.

2 Click the button for the email service or software you use (Gmail, Yahoo! Mail, and so on).

3 Enter your email address and (if necessary) password.

4 Click the Continue button.

5 If prompted to sign in to your email account, do so.

6 When LinkedIn displays how it would like to use your email information, click the Agree or Yes button.

Invitations

The people you select receive invitations to become connections. If they accept your invitation, you are added to each other's connections list.

(7) LinkedIn now displays all the people in your email contacts list who are also LinkedIn members. Check the names of those people you want to add to your LinkedIn connections list, or uncheck those names you don't want to add.

(8) Click the Add Connections button (or, if there isn't anyone to add, click Skip This Step).

(9) LinkedIn now recommends that you invite other email contacts to join LinkedIn. Check the names of those people you want to invite.

(10) Click the Add to Network button.

Receive and Reply to Private Messages

LinkedIn offers its own internal email system. This system enables you to send and receive messages to and from people you are connected to.

(1) From the LinkedIn menu bar, click the Messages icon to display your email Inbox. (If you have unread messages in your Inbox, the Messages item on the menu bar shows a number beside the Inbox text, indicating the number of unread messages waiting.)

2 A list of the people with whom you've most recently corresponded is displayed along the left side of the page; people with unread messages have a blue dot beside them. Click the person's name to read all messages to and from the selected person.

3 To delete all the messages in a conversation, click the X next to the person's name.

4 To reply to a message, click within the box beneath the message and start typing. Press Enter to send the message.

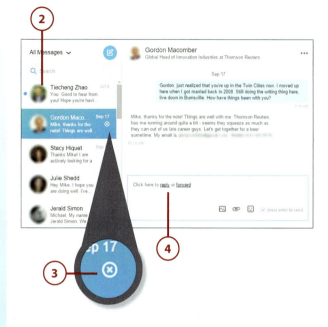

Compose a New Message

It is equally easy to send a new message to any of your LinkedIn connections.

1 From the LinkedIn menu bar, mouse over the Messages icon and then click the New icon. (Or, from the Inbox page, click the New icon.) This displays a new message page.

2 Enter the recipient's name or email address into the Type a Name box.

3 As you type, matching connections are displayed; click the name of the person you want to email.

4 Type your message into the Write Your Message box, and press Enter when done.

Post a Status Update

Like Facebook, LinkedIn enables users to post short status updates that are then displayed in their connections' home pages. (You can also publish longer "posts," but most people use the updates function.) Unlike Facebook, these status updates are not the main focus of the site; LinkedIn is still about personal connections and messages.

1 On the LinkedIn home page, click Share an Update. This expands the section to display a text box.

2 Click within the text box and type the text of your update.

3 To add a picture to this update, click the Upload a Photo icon and select the picture you want.

4 Click the Share With list and select how you want to share this update: Public, Just Your Connections, or Public + Twitter.

5 Click the Share button to post this update.

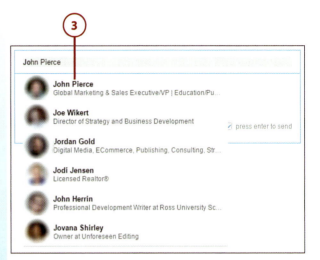

Using Pinterest

Pinterest (www.pinterest.com) is a newer social network with particular appeal to women—although there is a growing number of male users, too.

Unlike Facebook, which lets you post text-based status updates, Pinterest is all about images. The site consists of a collection of virtual online "pinboards" that people use to share pictures from the Web that they find interesting. Users "pin" photos and other images to their personal message boards and then share their pins with online friends. When you click a pin on Pinterest, you're taken to the original web page.

You can pin images of anything—clothing, furniture, recipes, do-it-yourself projects, and the like. Your Pinterest friends can then "repin" your images to their pinboards—and on and on.

Joining Pinterest

Like other social media sites, Pinterest is free to join and use. You can join (at www.pinterest.com) with your email address or by using your Facebook account login.

Create New Pinboards

Pinterest lets you create any number of pinboards, each dedicated to specific topics. If you're into quilting, you can create a Quilting board; if you're into radio-controlled airplanes, you can create an RC Airplanes board with pictures of your favorite craft.

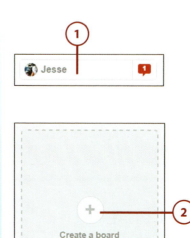

1. From the Pinterest home page (www.pinterest.com), click your name to display your profile page.

2. Click Create a Board to display the Create a Board panel.

(3) Enter the name for this board into the Name box.

(4) Enter a short description of this board into the Description box.

(5) Pull down the Category list and select a general category for this board.

(6) Ignore the Map, Keep It Secret?, and Collaborators options (unless you're working on a private project you don't want anyone else to see, such as assembling a list of gift ideas, in which case, click the Keep It Secret? option).

(7) Click the Create Board button.

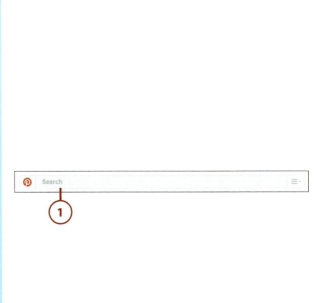

Find and Repin Interesting Items

Some people say that Pinterest is a little like a refrigerator covered with magnets holding up tons of photos and drawings. You can find a lot of interesting items pinned from other users—and then "repin" them to your own personal pinboards.

(1) Enter the name of something you're interested in into the Search box at the top of any Pinterest page and then press Enter. Pinterest displays pins that match your query.

2 Mouse over the item you want to repin and click the Pin It button. The Pick a Board panel displays.

3 Accept the previous user's description or add your own in the Description box.

4 Click the board you want to pin to. This pins the item to that board.

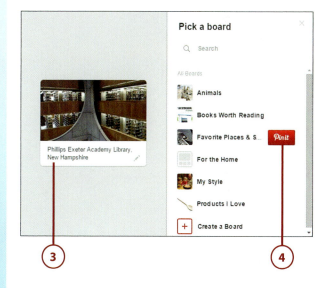

Pin an Item from a Web Page

You can also pin images you find on nearly any web page. It's as easy as copying and pasting the page's web address.

1 From any Pinterest page, click the + button in the lower-right corner.

2 Click Pin from a Website.

3 Enter the web address (URL) of the page you want to pin.

4 Click the Next button.

5 Pinterest now displays all images found on the selected web page. Mouse over the image you want to pin and click the Pin It button to open the Pick a Board panel.

6 Enter a short (500 characters or less) text description of or comment on this image in the Description box.

7 Click the board to which you want to pin this image. The item is now pinned to that board.

Not Always Welcome

Some websites don't want people to pin their images and code their pages to prohibit pinning. If you try to pin from one of these pages, you get a message that no pinnable images have been found. If you happen to pin an image that some entity owns and doesn't want you to pin, they can ask Pinterest to take down the pin. (Legally, Pinterest says it's not responsible for any copyright claims for items pinned to its site.)

>>>*Go Further*

PIN IT FROM YOUR BROWSER

It's even easier to pin an image from a web page if you install Pinterest's Browser Button in your web browser. When you click the + button and then select Pin from a Website, you see a link to get the Pinterest Browser Button. Click this link and you're taken to a page that describes the button. Click the Get Our Browser Button button, and the button is installed in your web browser—typically in the toolbar or next to the Address box.

When you next visit a web page that you want to pin from, click the Pinterest button in your browser. You see images from this web page; click the Pin It button for the image you want to pin and proceed from there.

Find People to Follow

When you find someone who posts a lot of things you're interested in, you can follow that person on Pinterest. Following a person means that all of that person's new pins display on your Pinterest home page.

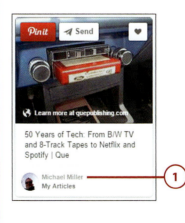

1. When you find a pin you like, click the name of the person who pinned it to see the board for that pin.

2. On the board page, click the person's name to see all of his boards.

3. Click the Follow button to follow all of this person's pins.

④ Alternatively, if you only want to follow pins to one of this person's boards, click the Follow button for the board you want to follow.

Using Twitter

Twitter is different from Facebook, LinkedIn, and Pinterest in that it's not a social network per se, but rather a microblogging service. Technicalities aside, Twitter is kind of like a Facebook but without the focus on picture sharing and groups and such. Instead, Twitter focuses on short (140-character) messages called *tweets*, which are shared with a user's followers.

As such, Twitter is immensely popular with younger users, but less so among 50+ users, who value the more social nature of Facebook and Pinterest. While there aren't a lot of 50 and over people who tweet, you may still want to join Twitter to follow the postings of your 20- and 30-something family members—or your favorite celebrities. (It's also good for getting up-to-the-minute news updates from major news organizations.)

Signing Up and Signing In

Like most other social media, Twitter is free. If you want to follow other users' tweets, as well as tweet yourself, you need to create an account, which you can do at www.twitter.com. Once you've signed up, you can sign in by returning to this page and entering your username and password.

Find Tweeters to Follow

You can follow any Twitter user. Unlike Facebook and LinkedIn, where friends and connections have to be mutually approved, you don't have to be approved to view another user's tweets. So if you want to follow Paul McCartney (@PaulMcCartney) or Fox News (@FoxNews) or just your neighbor down the street, you can do so without having to ask permission. (The only exception to this is if a user blocks you as a follower; any user can block any other user, which helps to cut down on online stalking.)

@name

Users on Twitter are identified by a username preceded by an at sign (@). So, for example, my username is **molehillgroup**, which translates into my Twitter "handle" of **@molehillgroup**.

There are several ways to find people to follow on Twitter. One approach is to accept the recommendations that Twitter makes, based on your past activities and interests. You can also search directly for specific users.

1 On the Twitter home page, go to the Who to Follow section and click View All. Twitter now displays its recommendations.

2 To view more about a person or organization, click that entity's name.

3 To follow this person or organization, click the Follow button.

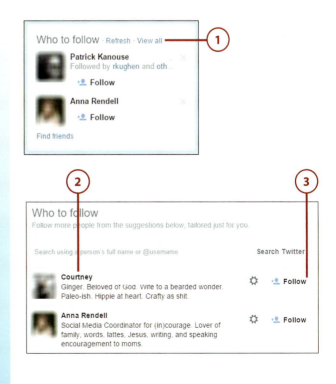

(4) To search for a person or organization on Twitter, enter the real name or Twitter username of the person or organization you want to follow into the Search box at the top right.

View Tweets

When you select other users to follow, you receive all their tweets on your Twitter home page. A tweet is a text-based post to the Twitter service. Each tweet must be 140 characters or less in length. Tweets can include images, videos, and links to other web pages.

(1) From the Twitter toolbar, click Home to display your home page.

(2) Tweets are listed in reverse chronological order, with the newest tweets at the top. The name of the sender and how long ago the tweet was made are listed at the top of each tweet. Scroll down the page to view older tweets.

(3) To view the profile summary for a given person, click that person's name or @name within the tweet.

(4) To "like" a tweet, mouse over the tweet and click the star (Favorite) icon.

5) To view other tweets on a highlighted topic, click the hashtag (#topic) within the tweet.

6) To view a web page linked to within a tweet, click the embedded URL.

7) Photos are embedded within tweets, but at a limited height. To view the full picture, click the photo.

8) To reply to a tweet, click the Reply icon. This opens a reply box beneath the original tweet; enter your reply into the box and then click the Tweet button.

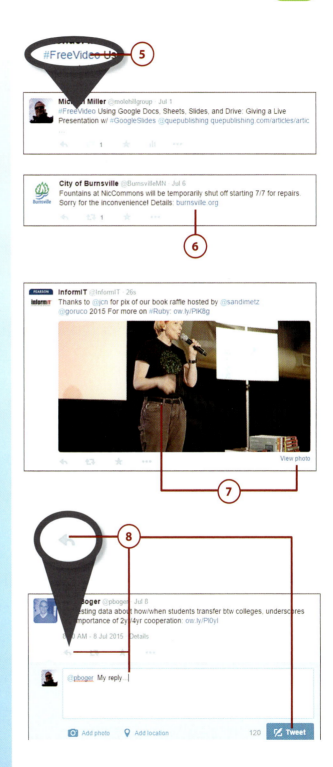

9 To retweet a tweet (that is, to resend the tweet to people who are following you), click the Retweet icon. This displays the Retweet This to Your Followers? panel.

10 Add any additional comments in the Add a Comment box.

11 Click the Retweet button.

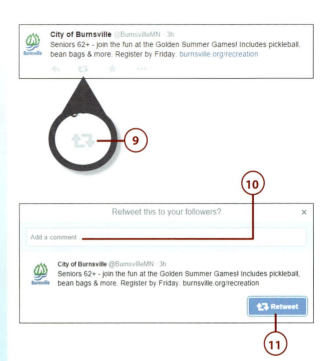

Post a Tweet

It's also easy to post your own tweets. Just know you need to stay within the 140-character limit.

1 From anywhere on the Twitter site, click the Tweet button on the toolbar. This displays the Compose a New Tweet panel.

2 Type your message into the large text box. Remember that a tweet can be no more than 140 characters in length. (There's a helpful character counter at the end of your tweet that lets you know how many character you have left to use.)

3 Click Add Photo to add a photo to your tweet.

4 Click the Tweet button.

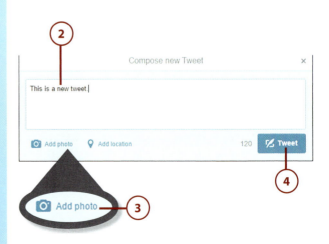

Web Links

To add a link to another website to your tweet, simply type the URL as part of your message. You may want to use a link-shortening service, such as bit.ly (www.bit.ly), to create shorter URLs to fit within Twitter's 140-character limit.

>>>*Go Further*
HASHTAGS AND MENTIONS

A *hashtag* is a word or phrase (with no spaces) in a tweet that is preceded by the hash or pound character, like this: **#hashtag**. Hashtags function much like keywords, by helping other users find relevant tweets when searching for a particular topic. A hashtag within a tweet is clickable; clicking a hashtag displays a list of the most recent tweets that include that word.

To include a hashtag in a tweet, just type a hash character or pound sign (#) before the word you want to reference, like this: **#keyword**.

You can also mention other users in your tweets. When you mention a person by username, that name becomes clickable by anyone viewing the tweet (and displays the user's profile summary). To include a mention, type an at sign (@) before the user's name, like this: **@username**.

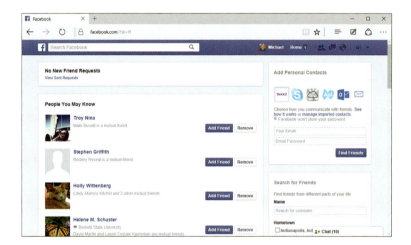

In this chapter, you learn how to reconnect with long-lost friends, as well as make new friends online.

→ Discovering Old Friends on Social Media

→ Searching for Friends on Google and Bing

→ Finding Friends on People Finder Sites

→ Making New Friends on Online Dating Sites

Finding Old Friends—And Making New Ones

The Internet is great for getting back in touch with old friends, schoolmates, and colleagues. You'd be surprised how much information about people ends up online—social network profiles and posts, local newspaper articles, comments on website message boards, even complete contact information. It's almost impossible for someone to escape visibility on the Web these days, which means if you know how and where to search, you can find practically anyone you're looking for.

The Internet is also great for making new friends—and meeting new potential love interests. Many Internet dating sites make it easy to find others who share your interests. Several of these are especially popular for those of us aged 50 and up.

So whether you want to get back in touch with someone from your past or meet someone new, all you need is an Internet connection and a web browser. Time to start looking!

Discovering Old Friends on Social Media

These days, everybody and their brother are on Facebook and other social media—which makes these social media great places to find just about anyone you're looking for. The two best social networks for finding 50+ users are Facebook and LinkedIn; the former because it's so big (1.5 billion users, remember), and the latter because it hones in on workplace connections.

Social Media

Learn more about Facebook and LinkedIn in Chapter 6, "Using Facebook and Other Social Media."

Find Friends on Facebook

Let's start with Facebook (www.facebook.com), which offers several different ways to find people who share some of your life experiences. You can search for people who came from your hometown, went to your high school or college, worked at the same companies you used to work for, and more.

(1) If you have a Find Friends button on the Facebook toolbar, click it. If not, click the Friends button to display the drop-down menu and then click Find Friends.

2 In the right column of the next page, scroll down until you see the Search for Friends panel. To search for someone by name, enter that person's name into the Name box.

3 To look for people who come from your hometown, go to the Hometown section and check your town. (If your hometown isn't listed, enter it into the text box first.)

4 To search for people who live near you now, go to the Current City section and check your city. (If your town or city isn't listed, enter it into the text box first.)

5 To search for people who went to the same high school you did, go to the High School section and check the name of your high school. (If your high school isn't listed, enter it into the text box first.)

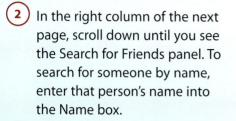

Search for Friends

Find friends from different parts of your life

Name

Search for someone — **2**

Hometown

☐ Indianapolis, Indiana — **3**

Enter another city

Current City

☐ Burnsville, Minnesota — **4**

Enter another city

High School

☐ Ben Davis High School — **5**

Enter another high school

6   To search for people who are already friends with your other Facebook friends, go to the Mutual Friend section and check the names of one or more friends. (If a particular friend isn't listed, enter his or her name into the text box first.)

7   To search for people who went to the same college or university you did, go to the College or University section and check the name of your school. (If your school isn't listed, enter its name into the text box first.)

8   To search for people who work or worked for one of your current or former employers, go to the Employer section and check the name of that company. (If a company isn't listed, enter its name into the text box first.)

9   To search for former classmates who went to the same graduate school you did (if, in fact, you went to graduate school), go to the Graduate School section and check the name of that school. (If your grad school isn't listed, enter its name into the text box first.)

6

Mutual Friend
- [ ] Jared Rendell
- [ ] Amy Elliott
- [ ] Kristi 'Elliott' Lee

   Enter another name

College or University
- [ ] Indiana University   **7**

   Enter another college or unive...

Employer
- [ ] The Molehill Group   **8**
- [ ] Macmillan Publishing

   Enter another employer

Graduate School

   Enter a college

9

10 Whichever options you select, Facebook now returns a list of suggested friends based on your selections. Click the Add Friend button to send a friend request to a specific person.

Multiple Filters

You can choose to filter your search on more than one criteria. For example, you can look for people who lived in your hometown and work at a given company, or who went to your college and live in your current city. Just select multiple options in the Search for Friends panel.

Find Colleagues on LinkedIn

LinkedIn (www.linkedin.com) is all about making business-related connections. As such, it's a great place to find former or current coworkers or others who work in your particular industry.

1 From the LinkedIn menu bar, click Advanced next to the Search box to display the Advanced People Search panel.

2 In the Relationship section, check how close a relationship you want to search for—1st Connections (people you know directly), 2nd Connections (people who know the people you know), and so forth.

3 To search for people still employed at a given company, click Current Company, click Add, and then enter the name of the company.

4 To search for people who were previously employed at a given company, click Past Company, click Add, and then enter the name of the company.

5 To search for people who went to the same school as you, click School, click Add, and then enter the name of the school.

6 Click the Search button. LinkedIn now displays people who match your search criteria.

7 Those with the closest connections to you are displayed first in the list. Click the Connect button for any person with whom you want to establish a connection.

People
Jobs

Advanced People Search

Keywords

First Name

Last Name

Title

Company

School

Location
Anywhere

Search   Reset

Relationship
- 1st Connections
- 2nd Connections
- Group Members
- 3rd + Everyone Else

Location

Current Company

Industry

Past Company

School

Profile Language

Nonprofit Interests

Vipul Redey 2nd
Director, Academics, Pearson Schools, India
Bengaluru Area, India · Education Management
• 1 shared connection · Similar
Current: Director, Academics at Pearson Education Services Private Lim...

Connect

David Camacho 2nd
Project Manager for México & Andean Region. Efficacy Champion.
CRM specialist.
Other · Information Technology and Services
• 1 shared connection · Similar
Current: Project Manager for México & Andean Region. Efficacy Champio...

Connect

Distant Connections

LinkedIn hides the names of people who have no shared connections with you. To contact these people, whomever they may be, you need to upgrade to a Premium membership.

Searching for Friends on Google and Bing

The Web's top search engines are also good places to find people you know or used to know. If someone has had any contact with the media, had papers published, even written comments to online message boards, chances are that Google and Bing know about it.

People searching on Google and Bing is as easy as any other type of search. Just enter the person's name into the search box and press Enter. You see a list of pages that contain that person's name.

Google and Bing

Learn more about searching with Google and Bing in Chapter 4, "Browsing and Searching the Web."

That said, most names are so common that the search engines return a lot of results that have nothing to do with the person you're looking for. Try it yourself by searching for me, **michael miller**. You see a lot of results for Michael Miller Fabrics, some for a lawyer named Michael Miller, and more for some doctors and scientists and teachers who share my name. Finding the real me amidst all the other listings that aren't me is difficult, if not impossible.

As such, you need to fine-tune your search by including more information about the person you're looking for. This means adding more keywords to the main search, so that search engines have more details to work with.

For example, if you're searching for me and know that I'm a writer, you could enter **michael miller writer**. Or if you know I live in Minnesota, enter **michael miller minnesota**. Of if you went to Ben Davis High School with me, enter

michael miller ben davis high school. Or if you know I used to be involved with model kit building, enter **michael miller model kit building**.

You get the point. The more information you know and enter about a person, the more likely it is that Google and Bing will find the right person on the Web.

>>>*Go Further*

TIPS FOR SEARCHING BY NAME

When you're searching for a person by name, there are a few tricks you can use to get better results. Try the following:

- **Search for an exact phrase.** Both Google and Bing return more accurate results when you tell them to search for an exact phrase—in this instance, a person's name. Surround the person's name with quotation marks, like this: **"michael miller"**. This tells the search engine to search only for instances where the two words appear together. Without the quotation marks, the search engine searches for pages that include the words **michael** and **miller**, not necessarily used together.

- **Include the middle initial.** There are many Michael Millers out there. There are fewer Michael L. Millers. Including a person's middle initial helps narrow your search results.

- **Consider all forms of a person's name.** If you're searching for Michael Miller, you may want to search for **mike miller**, **m miller**, and **mikey miller** in addition to my formal name. If the person you're looking for has a nickname, search for that, as well.

- **Search for the person's spouse or other relatives.** If you know the name of your friend's husband or wife, search for him or her, too. For that matter, try searching for a person's siblings or parents or children; if you can get in touch with a relative, they can help you get in touch with the person you're looking for.

- **Search for a woman's maiden and married names.** Searching for a woman is particularly problematic, as you may know her maiden name but not her married name. Search using whatever information you have, but know that she may be going by another name that you don't know.

In short, use your imagination and whatever information you know to better find anyone you're looking for. Simple name-only searches may not cut it.

Finding Friends on People Finder Sites

Searching via Google and Bing is easy and free, but sometimes returns results that are just too broad. You may have better luck using a dedicated people finder site—that is, a website devoted solely to finding people (and their addresses and phone numbers, in many instances).

A number of people finder sites are available online. Some are free to use; others require you to pay to access full search results. We look at a half-dozen of the most popular people finder sites.

AnyWho

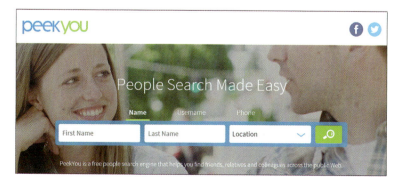

AnyWho (www.anywho.com) is a free site that searches public and commercial records, along with other publicly available information. You can search by name, address, or phone number. The site returns address and phone number.

PeekYou

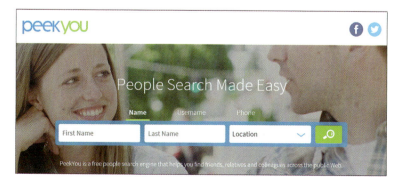

PeekYou (www.peekyou.com) is a good site for finding people who have an active Internet or social network presence. It's a semi-free site that searches social networks and search engines and attempts to index people and their links on the Web. (Clicking web links is free; PeekYou charges for viewing public data.) You can search by name, location, social network username, or phone number. The site returns other social network usernames, work information, interests, personal websites, and more.

Spokeo

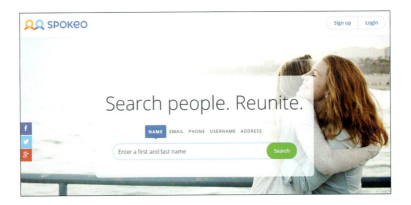

Spokeo (www.spokeo.com) requires a paid membership. It searches public records, white pages listings, and social networks. You can search by name, location, email address, phone number, street address, or social network username; the site returns address, phone number, email address, marital status, known relatives, and more.

That'sThem

That'sThem (www.thatsthem.com) is a free site that returns a lot of interesting information you don't find on other sites. It searches social networks, consumer data, public records, and more. You can search by name, location, email address, phone number, automobile VIN, or social network username. The site returns address, phone number, education, occupation, automobiles owned, estimated income, and more. (I find this one of the more useful people finder sites.)

White Pages

White Pages (www.whitepages.com) is a free site that does just what its name implies—it searches basic white pages information. You can search by name, phone number, or address. The site returns address, phone number, age, and relatives.

Zabasearch

Zabasearch (www.zabasearch.com) is a free site that searches public records databases. You can search by name and location. The site returns address and phone number.

>>>*Go Further*

SEARCH PUBLIC RECORDS

Federal, state, county, and local governments are putting more and more of their public records online—which means you can find a lot of this information by searching the relevant websites. Depending on the municipality and what's put online, you can often find court records, property records, tax records, criminal records, and the like.

You can use Google or Bing to find the appropriate online records offered by your state, county, or city. Or you can go to USA.gov (www.usa.gov), which lets you search government records from across the country. Just enter the person's name and select what type of records you're searching for.

Know, however, that the availability and quality of public records vary significantly by location. Larger, more heavily populated locations are more likely to have more robust public records searches. Smaller or less populated municipalities may not even offer online public records searches.

In addition, you should be cautious of people finder sites that search public records (especially court and criminal records) and charge you a hefty fee for doing so. Sites such as InstantCheckmate, Intelius, and PeopleFinders charge up to $50 for reports that you can assemble yourself from public records. Granted, these sites make it easy to gather this information, but you can save a ton of money by getting it yourself. (Plus, if you're searching for an old friend, do you really want or need to find his or her criminal history?)

Making New Friends on Online Dating Sites

The heck with old friends. There comes a time when you want to make new friends—for dating, romance, and such. Not surprisingly, a number of online dating sites want to help you connect, and some of them specifically target 50+ users.

Note that most legitimate dating sites charge for at least some of their services. You typically sign up on a monthly (and sometimes weekly) basis, so make sure you cancel your subscription when you find someone you want to spend some time with.

When you join an online dating site, you create a profile that other users can see. Enter the relevant information about yourself, including physical details (age, height, hair color, and so forth) as well as other personal information—your hobbies, likes, dislikes, you name it. Also upload a decent photo of yourself. You want to try to make yourself attractive to potential partners, but without misrepresenting yourself or stretching the truth too much.

The following online dating sites are particularly popular among singles 50 and over. Give one a try and see what kind of people you can find there.

>>>Go Further

FINDING FRIENDS TO DO THINGS WITH

You can also use the Internet to find others who can get together with you to participate in various types of fun activities. Whether you're looking for someone to accompany you to the theater, take a class together, attend a book club meeting, play a game of golf, or just hang out and talk, you can find interesting people via the web. Check out sites like GroupSpaces (www.groupspaces.com), MEETin (www.meetin.org), and Meetup (www.meetup.com) to find others who share your interests.

eHarmony Senior Dating

eHarmony is one of the largest online dating sites, period. (You've probably seen their commercials on TV.) The site has more than 20 million registered users, with 15,000 new users signing up each day. eHarmony has a special section of its site devoted to "senior singles," located at www.eharmony.com/senior-dating. The gender ratio runs 52/48 female/male.

When you sign up, you answer 258 multiple-choice questions that help to fine-tune your profile on the site. (Yes, 258 questions. Yeesh!) eHarmony then uses your answers to recommend the best matches. You actually don't search for partners on the site; you wait for eHarmony to make the matches for you.

As to membership, eHarmony isn't cheap; in fact, it's one of the pricier services out there. A one-month membership costs $59.95. Sign up (and pay in advance) for a longer period and the per-month cost goes down; for example, a 12-month membership runs $25.95 per month.

Match.com

eHarmony's chief rival is Match.com (www.match.com), with more than 20 million members—10 percent or so who identify themselves as "seniors." Match.com doesn't have a specific part of the site for 50+ users, but it's easy enough to specify an appropriate age range you're looking for. (In fact, the Match.com user base skews almost 20 years older than does eHarmony's.) The gender ratio runs 51/49 female/male.

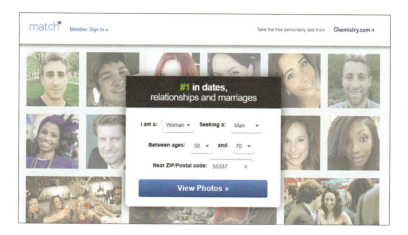

Match.com is a more traditional site than eHarmony. You create your own personal profile, of course, but then you browse through or search others' profiles until you find one you like. You can then contact that member directly and get to know each other on a one-to-one basis.

You can browse Match.com profiles for free, but if you want to contact anybody, you need a membership. A one-month membership costs $41.99, but as with eHarmony, that rate goes down with longer memberships. For example, a 12-month prepaid membership runs $20.99 per month.

OKCupid

With about 3.5 million total users, OKCupid (www.okcupid.com) is about a fifth the size of eHarmony and Match.com but still a popular dating site for 50+ users. You create your profile by answering a series of questions, which is easy enough to do. (Tip: Answer only those questions you want—and ignore those targeted more at younger users.)

Unlike the other services, OKCupid is free. On one hand, free is good. On the other hand, free means you find more people who are less invested in and serious about the whole endeavor. In other words, you're likely to find a larger number of lower-quality matches on OKCupid compared to other online dating sites. You get what you pay for.

OurTime

OurTime (www.ourtime.com) is an online dating site devoted exclusively to people 50 and over. OurTime claims 1.4 million members, and they're all our age and looking for others our age. The gender ratio is fairly balanced, at 52/48 female/male.

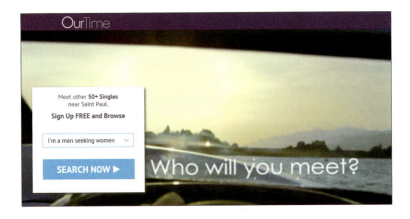

Like the other sites, you answer a series of multiple-choice questions to create your profile. (You're also encouraged to add some longer personal content, too—kind of like essay questions.) You can then browse or search the profiles for potential matches.

You can browse for free but have to join up and pay to contact anybody. A one-month membership costs $23.99; sign up for a six-month membership and that prices goes down to $11.99/month.

SeniorPeopleMeet

SeniorPeopleMeet (www.seniorpeoplemeet.com) is another dating site for mature folks. It's targeted at singles aged 55 and up, and claims to be "the #1 dating community for seniors." Know, however, that the gender ratio is skewed heavily toward women, at 59/41 female/male. (That's good for older guys, I guess.)

Creating a profile is as simple as answering the requisite questions and uploading a photo. You can search for matches by age, location, gender, and profile features. (More advanced searches are available too, if you like.)

Browsing is free, but you need to pay to contact other members. You pay $29.95 for a one-month membership, or $11.99 per month if you sign up for a six-month membership.

Dating After 50

Learn more about dating (online and off) for older singles in the book *Dating After 50 for Dummies*. It's available at retailers nationwide.

>>>Go Further

LET'S BE CAREFUL OUT THERE

When you're doing the online dating thing, know that you can run into people who aren't quite who they say they are. There are people who misrepresent themselves to appear more appealing (age fudging is common), folks who are browsing with no intention of ever starting a relationship, scammers who like to prey on lonely single people, and even the occasional crazy who can physically harm you. How do you make online dating safer?

First, know that not everyone is who they say they are. Take everything you read online with a grain of salt, and don't get all excited about someone until you've had an opportunity to know that person better.

Second, keep your guard up. Be aware of anyone trying to gain your sympathy and scam you out of money. Never, ever, *ever* give or send money to anyone you meet online. Don't write a check, don't make a wire transfer, don't provide bank account or credit card information. Make whomever it is you're with pay their own way—both before and after you meet in public.

Along the same lines, don't share your personal information with someone you've just met (or even dated for a while). Don't give them your social security number, birth date, online passwords, even your address and phone number. Keep your personal information private. (And guard your personal contact information until you've really gotten to know someone.)

Be cautious of anyone who immediately wants to take things "live," by chatting online, going to personal email, or talking on the phone. Give things time to develop before getting personal. Anyone who wants to go "private" too quickly is probably out to get you.

When it comes time to meet someone in person, you need to take reasonable precautions. First, always meet in public, never at a person's home or in your home—and never in a remote location. Second, tell a friend where and when you're going, and have them call you midway through the meeting. (That means taking your mobile phone with you, of course.) Third, keep your wits about you; if you're drinking, take it easy and stay sober. Finally, provide your own transportation, even if it's arranging a taxi; you want to have your own ride home in case things don't work out.

Bottom line, trust your instincts. When meeting new people online, it's better to be cautious, paranoid even, than naïve. Yes, you may be a trusting person, but online you need to verify and then trust. If something doesn't feel quite right, then back away. Proceed with caution, and you just might meet someone worth dating.

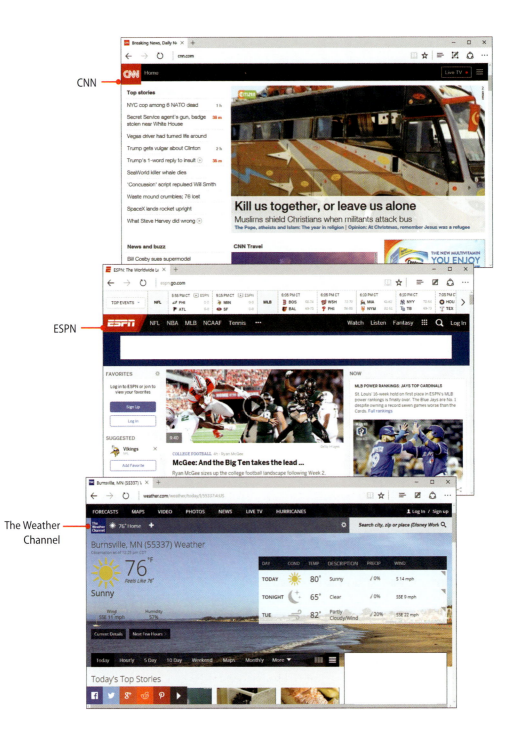

CNN

ESPN

The Weather
Channel

8

Finding News, Sports, and Weather Online

You can get just about all the information you want on the Web—local and national (and international) news, sports scores and stories, current weather and future forecasts, even stock prices and financial analysis. And when you get your news and other information online, it's almost always up-to-the-minute up-to-date. Information on the Web is continuously updated, so you can find out what's happening pretty much as it happens. You don't have to wait around for the nightly news report, the morning newspaper, or the weekly newsmagazine. Just fire up your web browser and see what's happening now!

Reading the News Online

The Internet has become a primary source of news in today's digital world. We might have grown up reading newspapers and magazines, but readers today are more likely to get their news and information online. In fact, most newspapers and magazines have their own online editions—often readable for free.

National and International News

Let's start with the big news sites that offer a mix of national and international news—often with a dash of political commentary thrown in. If you only bookmark one news site in your browser, it'll probably be one of these.

1 All the major television news networks have robust websites. For example, ABC News (abcnews.go.com) offers U.S., world, political, and entertainment news in both text and video stories.

2 CBS News (www.cbsnews.com) also offers current and breaking news from its worldwide news gathering organization. Sections include U.S., World, Politics, Entertainment, Health, MoneyWatch, SciTech, Crime, Sports, and more.

3 One of the biggest and most popular news sites online comes from the CNN (www.cnn.com) cable news network. You find a combination of text stories, video reports, and streaming live video. Sections include U.S., World, Politics, Tech, Health, Entertainment, Living, Travel, Money, and Sports.

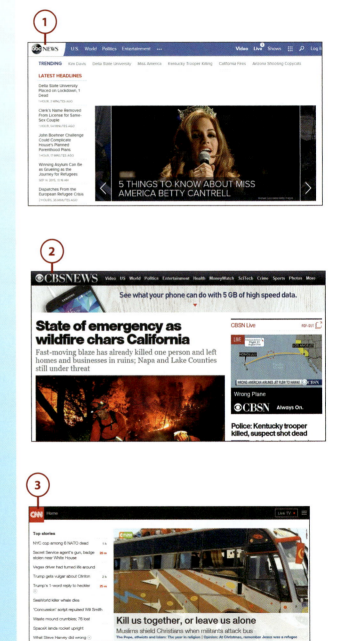

4 FOX News (www.foxnews.com) reports from the conservative side of the political aisle with a surprisingly robust website. You find similar coverage here as on the CNN site, but with more conservative political commentary. Sections include Politics, U.S., Opinion, Entertainment, Tech, Science, Health, Travel, Lifestyle, World, and Sports. This site offers lots of video reports and live streaming, too.

5 NBC News (www.nbcnews.com) offers similar content to the ABC and CBS sites, but with a little more political commentary from its sibling MSNBC network. (MSNBC is also online, at www.msnbc.com, but with less general news coverage.) Sections include U.S., World, Local, Politics, Health, Tech, Science, Pop Culture, Business, Investigations, Sports, and more.

Newspapers Online

The big national newspapers also have good and popular websites. Chief among them are *The New York Times* (www.nytimes.com), *USA Today* (www.usatoday.com), *The Wall Street Journal* (www.wsj.com), and *The Washington Post* (www.washingtonpost.com). Know, however, that some of these sites require paid subscriptions to view all available content.

Local News

The big national news sites are great but don't offer much, if anything, in the way of local news. When you want to find out what's happening down the street, you need to turn to local media websites.

1 One of the best sources of local news is your local newspaper. Use Google or Bing to search for your local newspaper online, or go to the US Newspaper List (www.usnpl.com) for a list of newspapers nationwide.

2 Many local television and radio stations also have websites with up-to-date local news, sports, and weather information. Search Google or Bing for radio and TV station sites in your area. (For example, to search for TV stations in Orlando, query **Orlando tv stations**.)

3 Patch (www.patch.com) is a consortium of neighborhood news websites. Enter your ZIP Code to view news and information gathered locally by neighborhood correspondents. (Patch is available for more than 900 communities in 23 states but does not yet have full nationwide coverage.)

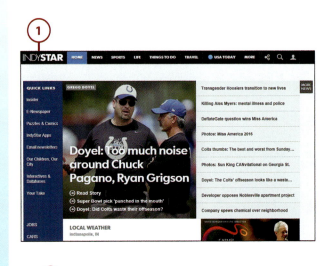

Online Subscriptions

Many local newspapers have free online editions, although some charge for online access. You might get free or discounted online access as part of your print subscription, however, so ask about available options. Some paid newspaper sites also let you view a limited number of articles at no charge, even without a sub-scription.

>>>*Go Further*
KEEPING IN TOUCH WHEREVER YOU ARE

You're not limited to reading the local news from where you currently reside. If you're vacationing elsewhere, doing the snowbird thing during the winter, or just curious about what's happening where you grew up, you can use the Internet to access those local news sites from wherever you happen to be.

For example, if your current home is in Minnesota but you winter in Florida, use Google to search for your local Minneapolis newspaper or television station, and then read your northern news while you're sunning in the South. Likewise, if you grew up in Indiana but now live in Arizona, there's nothing stopping you from reading *The Indianapolis Star* online in your web browser.

You can even read news from other countries online. If your family has Irish roots, for example, just search Google for newspapers in Ireland and keep in touch from around the globe.

Keeping Up with Your Favorite Sports Online

If you're a sports fan, you're in luck. There are tons of fun, useful, and informative sports sites on the Internet. Whether you're looking for the latest scores and stats or more in-depth reporting, you can find it online.

Sports Portals

The best sports sites on the Web resemble the best news sites— they're actually portals to all sorts of content and services, including up-to-the-minute scores, post-game recaps, in-depth reporting, and much more. If you're looking for sports information online, one of these portals is the place to start.

1. All the major broadcast networks offer significant sports coverage and in turn have robust sports-oriented websites. In particular, check out CBS Sports (www.cbssports.com), FOXSports (www.foxsports.com), and NBC Sports (www.nbcsports.com).

2. The largest and most popular sports-related site on the Web comes from the good folks at the ESPN cable network. The ESPN website (espn.go.com) offers coverage of every major sport—and many minor ones. You find scores, stats, and stories for professional football, baseball, basketball, tennis, auto racing, golf, and more. There's college coverage, too, and many videos to watch.

3 Sports Illustrated (www.si.com), the venerable sports magazine, offers an equally informative website. There's coverage of all major professional and college sports, from current scores to more in-depth reporting.

Major League Sports Sites

Each of the major sports leagues runs its own official website. Here you find team info, player stats, and the opportunity to deplete your wallet by purchasing all sorts of official league and team merchandise.

1 Follow your favorite major league baseball teams and players at the MLB.com website (www.mlb.com). You find scores, stats, standings, and schedules, as well as a lot of video highlights.

2 If you're a basketball fan, follow your favorite NBA teams at www.nba.com. There's the requisite combination of scores, stats, standings, and stories; you can also buy game tickets on the site.

3 If you follow women's basket-ball, check out the WNBA website (www.wnba.com). You find news stories, statistics, standings, and more at this full-featured site.

4 Football fans will appreciate the NFL's website (www.nfl.com). You get the expected scores, stats, and standings, as well as all the information you need to run your own fantasy football team.

5 The National Hockey League website (www.nhl.com) is the place to go if you're a big hockey fan. All the expected game and player information is present.

College Sports

If you're interested in college sports, a good place to start is NCAA Online, at www.ncaa.org. This site offers news, statistics, and an online hall of champions.

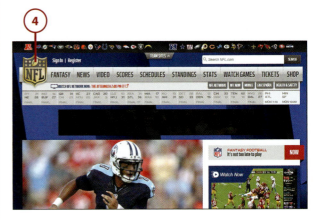

6 Golfers will appreciate the PGA website (www.pga.com). Not only can you follow your favorite golfers and tournaments, there's also golf instruction and tips, as well as detailed information about golf courses around the world.

Getting Weather Forecasts Online

Weather reports and forecasts are readily available on the Web; most of the major news portals and local websites offer some variety of weather-related services. There are also, however, a number of dedicated weather sites online.

Weather Portals

The Web's major weather portals offer a combination of local and national forecasts, weather radar, satellite maps, and more.

1 AccuWeather (www.accuweather.com) is a popular general weather website. Enter your location for local conditions and forecasts.

2 The Weather Channel's website (www.weather.com) is one of the most detaviled in terms of local weather forecasts and conditions. You can view hourly, daily, weekly, and long-term forecasts, as well as view current conditions on an interactive radar map.

3 WeatherNation (www. weathernationtv.com) is a relative newcomer to the online weather scene but offers a robust website with a combination of local weather, national weather, weather news, and interactive weather maps.

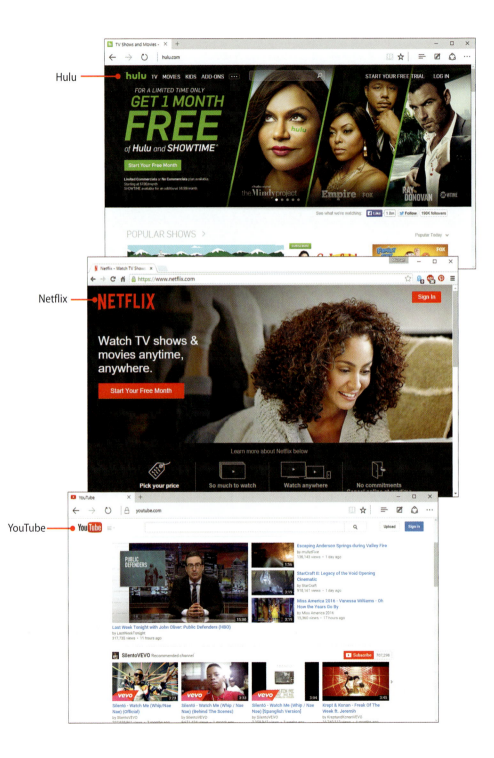

Hulu

Netflix

YouTube

→ Watching Movies and TV on Netflix

→ Watching TV Shows on Hulu

→ Viewing and Sharing Videos on YouTube

9

Watching Movies, TV Shows, and Videos Online

You and I grew up watching a black and white television set that received three (maybe four) channels. If we wanted to watch a movie, we went down to the local movie theater. There weren't a couple of hundred channels on cable TV, and we couldn't purchase movies on videotape or DVD.

It's all different today. Thanks to the Internet, just about any TV show or movie you want is available online, for viewing on your computer, tablet, or smartphone. While you can purchase and download videos for future viewing, most people today use streaming video services such as Netflix and Hulu to watch whatever they want, whenever they want it.

Whether you are looking for the latest episode of *Dancing with the Stars*, a classic Humphrey Bogart movie, or that latest "viral video" you've been hearing about, all you need is a relatively fast broadband Internet connection and a web browser. Oh, and maybe a little popcorn, too.

Watching Movies and TV on Netflix

You can watch all the movies and TV shows you want for a low $9.99/month subscription on Netflix (www.netflix.com). Netflix offers a mix of both classic and newer movies, as well as a surprising number of classic and newer television programs. There's something to please just about everyone.

Other Streaming Video Services

While Netflix is the market-leading streaming video service, there are other similar services online you might want to check out. These include Amazon Video (www.amazon.com/video), Crackle (www.crackle.com), and Sling TV (www.sling.com).

Watch a Program on Netflix

You can watch Netflix from any web browser on your computer, or from its mobile app for tablets and smartphones. You need to sign up for a subscription, of course, and then sign in to your account. From there, it's just a matter of finding the program (movie or TV show) you want to watch.

1. In your web browser, go to www.netflix.com and sign in. If you've created multiple viewers in your account, click to select who's viewing.

2. Scroll down to view videos in different categories—Popular on Netflix, Trending Now, Top Picks, and such.

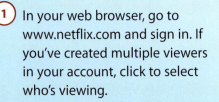

3 Click Browse to display the different genres available.

4 Click a genre to view movies or shows of that type.

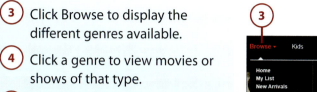

5 To search for a specific movie or show, click Search to expand the Search box.

6 Enter the name of the movie or show into the Search box and then press Enter.

7 When you find a movie or show you want to watch, mouse over it and click the down arrow. The detail pane for that movie or show displays.

8 If you selected a television show, click Episodes.

9 Click the Seasons control and select which season of the show you want to watch.

10 Click to play a particular episode.

11 If you selected a movie, click the Play button on the image to watch that movie.

12 Netflix begins playing the movie or show you selected. Right-click anywhere on the screen to display the playback controls.

13 Click the Fullscreen button at the lower right to display the movie fullscreen.

14 Click the Pause button to pause playback; the Pause button changes to a Play button. Click the Play button to resume playback.

15 Click and drag the scrub (slider) control to move directly to another part of the movie.

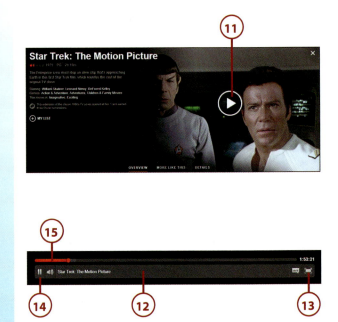

>>>Go Further
NETWORK TV PROGRAMMING

Most major broadcast and cable TV networks offer their shows for viewing from their websites. Most are free; some (such as HBO GO) are not. These include the following:

- ABC (abc.go.com)
- AMC (www.amc.com)
- CBS (www.cbs.com)
- Comedy Central (www.comedycentral.com)

- CW (www.cwtv.com)
- Food Network (www.foodnetwork.com)
- Fox (www.fox.com)
- HBO (www.hbogo.com)
- MeTV (www.metvnetwork.com)

- NBC (www.nbc.com)
- Nick (www.nick.com)
- Showtime (www.sho.com)
- TCM (www.tcm.com)
- TNT (www.tntdrama.com)
- USA Network (www.usanetwork.com)

In addition, you can get your daily sports fix via the streaming videos offered on the ESPN website (espn.go.com).

Watching TV Shows on Hulu

Netflix is great for watching movies and classic TV shows, but Hulu is a better service for newer television programming. Hulu offers episodes from a number of major-network TV shows, as well as some new and classic feature films. (There is also a fair number of programs from Canada, England, and other countries.) The standard free membership offers access to a limited number of videos; pay $7.99/month to view a larger selection of newer shows.

Watch TV Programs on Hulu

You can use any web browser to watch programs on the Hulu website. Just go to www.hulu.com and create a new account or log in to an existing account.

1. Hulu's home page displays a variety of featured programs. Scroll down to view recommended programming by type.

2. To view television programs, click TV at the top of the page.

3 To view programs by genre, click the Genres tile.

4 To search for a specific show, enter the name of the show into the top-of-page Search box and then press Enter.

5 Click the tile for the show you want to watch.

6 When the detailed program page appears, scroll down to view available episodes, clips, and extras.

7 To view seasons by episode, click Available Seasons and then click the season you want. (This option is not shown if only one season is available.)

8 Click the tile for the episode you want to watch.

9 Hulu begins playing the program you selected. Move your mouse over the screen to display the playback controls.

10 Click the Pause button to pause playback; the Pause button changes to a Play button. Click the Play button to resume playback.

11 Click and drag the scrub (slider) control to move directly to another part of the program.

12 Click the Fullscreen button to view the program fullscreen on your computer display. (Press Esc to exit fullscreen mode.)

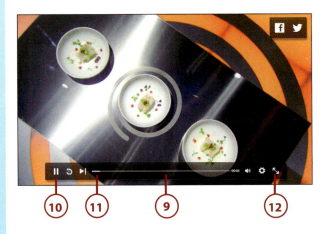

Movies

Hulu also offers a variety of movies for online viewing. The standard free membership has a very limited selection of movie programming, typically documentaries and movie trailers. The $7.99 premium membership offers a much larger selection of movies.

Viewing and Sharing Videos on YouTube

Netflix and Hulu are both popular, but the *most* popular video site on the Web is YouTube. This site is a video-sharing community; users can upload their own videos and watch videos uploaded by other members.

Although YouTube doesn't have nearly as many movies or TV shows as the other video sites, it does have more videos in total—many of them uploaded by members of the site. YouTube is where you find all those homemade videos of cute cats and laughing babies that everybody's watching. (You also find many educational and how-to videos, as well as music videos and clips from old TV shows.)

When you find a video you like, you can share it with your friends and family. This is how a video goes "viral," as it's shared from user to user.

View a Video

You access YouTube from any web browser. Unlike the commercial video services we've discussed, you use YouTube for free—no subscription necessary.

Movies on YouTube

In addition to its user-uploaded videos, YouTube offers a variety of commercial movies. Some movies are free; others can be rented on a 48-hour pass for as low as $1.99.

1 From within your web browser, go to the YouTube site at www.youtube.com.

2 To search for a particular video, enter what you're looking for into the Search box and then press Enter or click the Search (magnifying glass) button.

3 Click the video you want to watch.

4 The video begins playing automatically when the video page displays.

5 Click the Pause button to pause playback; click the button again to resume playback.

6 Click the Fullscreen button to view the video on your entire computer screen. (Press Esc to exit fullscreen mode.)

7 Click the thumbs-up button to "like" the video. (You need to be signed in to a YouTube account to perform this action.)

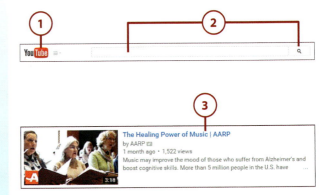

>>>Go Further

SHARING VIDEOS

Find a video you think a friend would like? YouTube makes it easy to share any video with others (as long as you're signed in to a YouTube account, that is).

Click the Share button under the video player to display the Share panel. You can then opt to email a link to the video, post the video to your Facebook feed, or tweet a link to the video on Twitter.

Upload Your Own Video

If you take movies with your camcorder or smartphone, you can transfer those movies to your computer and then upload them to YouTube. This is a great way to share your home videos with friends and family online. (Note that you have to be signed in to a YouTube or Google account to upload videos.)

Uploading from a Smartphone

If you shoot video with your smartphone or tablet, you may be able to upload to YouTube directly from your device or the YouTube mobile app. Check your device or app to see what's available.

1 Click the Upload button at the top of any YouTube page.

2 Click Select Files to Upload to display the Open dialog box.

Upload —①

Select files to upload

Or drag and drop video files

Public ▼

3 Navigate to and select the video file you want to upload.

4 Click the Open button.

5 As the video is uploaded, YouTube displays the video information page. Enter a title for the video into the Title box.

6 Enter a description for the video into the Description box.

7 Enter one or more keywords to describe the video into the Tags box.

8 Select a thumbnail for the video.

9 Click the Publish button to make your video live.

Thumbnail

After the video is done uploading, you may be prompted to select a thumbnail image for it. This thumbnail is displayed on all search results pages where your video appears.

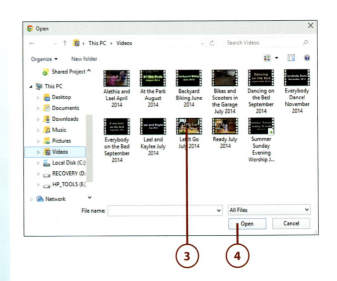

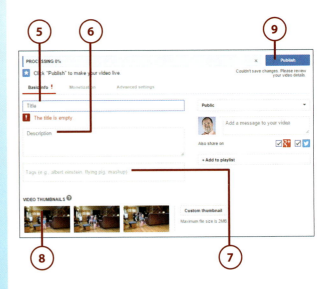

iHeartRadio

Pandora

Spotify

TuneIn

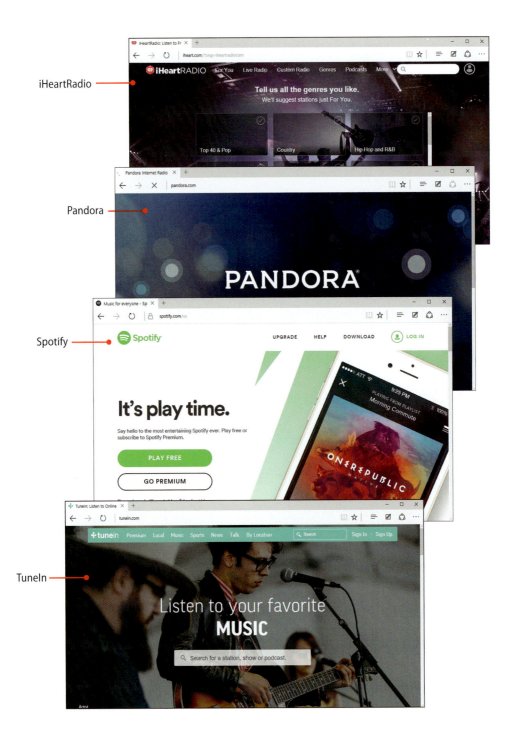

In this chapter, you learn how to use the Internet to listen to your favorite music.

→ Listening to Streaming Music Services
→ Listening to Local Radio Stations Online

Listening to Music Online

If you're like me, you grew up listening to music on the radio (AM first, then FM), and on vinyl records—both 45s and LPs. Well, that world is long gone. Radio is still around, although the old everything-goes Top 40 format has been supplanted by narrow niches for genres you've never heard of. Vinyl records, however, have been supplanted first by compact discs, then by digital downloads, and now by streaming music services. The music's still there, you just get it in different ways.

The Internet plays a big part in how we listen to music today. With your computer (or mobile device) and an Internet connection, you can find just about any song or album ever recorded and play the music on that same device. Streaming music services like Pandora and Spotify function much like old-fashioned radio stations, but with a little more personalization. And you can listen to traditional AM and FM radio online, too, at the iHeartRadio and TuneIn sites.

Listening to Streaming Music Services

People our age have been conditioned to purchase the music we like, whether on vinyl, cassette tape, compact disc, or via digital download. But there's an entire world of music on the Internet that you don't have to purchase. It's called *streaming music*, and it gives you pretty much all you can listen to for a low monthly subscription price—or even for free. There's nothing to download; the music is streamed to your computer in real time over the Internet.

The two largest streaming music services are Pandora and Spotify. You access both of these services from any web browser.

>>>*Go Further*

ON-DEMAND VERSUS PERSONALIZED SERVICES

There are two primary types of streaming music services on the Internet. The first model, typified by Pandora, is like traditional radio in that you can't dial up specific tunes; you have to listen to whatever the service beams out, but in the form of personalized playlists or virtual radio stations. The second model, typified by Spotify, lets you specify which songs you want to listen to; we call these *on-demand services*.

Listen to Pandora

Pandora is much like traditional AM or FM radio in that you listen to the songs Pandora selects for you along with accompanying commercials. It's a little more personalized than traditional radio, however, in that you create your own custom stations. All you have to do is choose a song or artist; Pandora then creates a station with other songs like the one you picked. You access Pandora from your web browser, at www.pandora.com, or via the Pandora mobile app on your smartphone or tablet.

Free versus Paid

Pandora's basic membership is free but ad supported. (You have to suffer through commercials.) To get rid of the commercials, pay for the $4.99/month Pandora One subscription.

1. On your initial visit to the Pandora website (www.pandora.com) you're prompted to create your first radio station. On subsequent visits, enter the name of a song, genre, artist, or composer into the Create Station box at the top-left corner and then press Enter. This creates a new station based on your selection.

2. The new station is added to your station list on the left side of the page. Click a station to begin playback; information about this track and artist is now displayed.

3. To pause playback, click the Pause button at the top of the page. Click Play to resume playback.

4. To like the current song, click the thumbs up button. This tells Pandora to play more songs like this one.

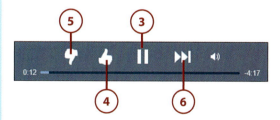

5. If you don't like the current song, click the thumbs down button. Pandora skips to the next song, does not play the current song again, and plays fewer songs like it.

6. To skip to the next song without disliking the current song, click the next track button.

Listen to Spotify

The other big streaming music service is Spotify. Unlike Pandora, Spotify lets you choose specific tracks to listen to.

Spotify offers a web-based version you can access via your web browser and a standalone app that offers enhanced functionality. We talk about the Spotify app here, as it's more full-featured, so go to Spotify's website (www.spotify.com) and click Get Spotify to download it. (There's also a Spotify mobile app for your tablet or smartphone; we're talking about the computer app here.)

Free versus Paid

Spotify's basic membership is free, but you're subjected to commercials every few songs. If you want to get rid of the commercials (and get on-demand music on your mobile devices, too), you need to pay for a $9.99/month subscription.

1. Open the Spotify app and then click Genres & Moods to browse by musical genre.

2. Click a genre tile to view music of that type.

3. To search for a specific song, album, or artist, enter your query into the top-of-page Search box and then press Enter.

4. Click a playlist, album, or artist to view all included songs.

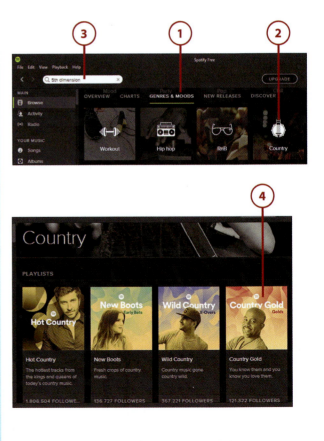

5 Click the green Play button to play all the songs in the playlist or album, or by that artist.

6 Click a song title to play that particular track.

7 Use the playback controls at the bottom left to pause, rewind, or fast-forward playback, or to raise or lower the volume.

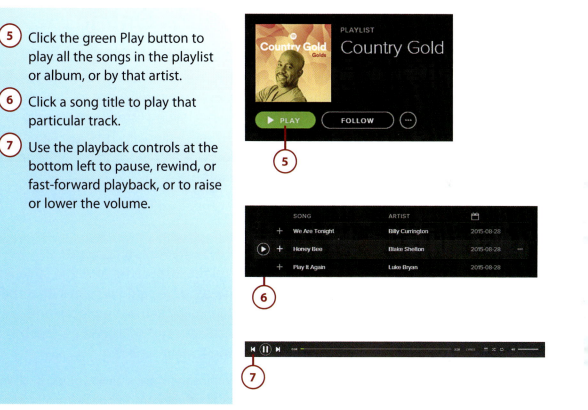

>>>Go Further

OTHER STREAMING MUSIC SERVICES

Pandora and Spotify aren't the only streaming music services on the Internet. You can check out and listen to any of these popular streaming music services using your web browser:

- Apple Music (www.apple.com/music/)
- Google Play Music All Access (play.google.com/about/music/)
- Groove Music (music.microsoft.com)
- Rhapsody (www.rhapsody.com)
- Slacker (www.slacker.com)

Listening to Local Radio Stations Online

If you'd rather just listen to your local AM or FM radio station—or to a radio station located in another city—you can do that over the Internet, too. While many individual stations have their own websites and mobile apps for listening live, two other services—iHeartRadio and TuneIn—let you listen to practically any radio station in the United States and many more globally. This way you can keep in touch with your local stations when you're away from home—or listen to the best of the best from anywhere in the world!

Listen to iHeartRadio

iHeartRadio is a streaming audio service owned by media conglomerate iHeartMedia (formerly Clear Channel). As you might suspect, iHeartRadio streams more than 800 iHeartMedia stations and hundreds more stations from across the country. Because of the iHeartMedia connection, many competing local radio stations don't offer their programming to iHeartRadio, giving listeners a much smaller selection of stations than the competing TuneIn service.

iHeartRadio is available as a free mobile app for smartphones and tablets, and on your computer at www.iheart.com. Listening is free, although you want to create your own personal account.

1. Go to the iHeartRadio website (www.iheart.com) and sign up or sign in to your free account. The main page displays your favorite and recommended stations. Click a station to listen to it.

2. To search for a specific station, enter that station's call letters or location into the Search box and press Enter.

3 To browse for stations in a given city, click the Live Radio tab. From here you can select the country, metropolitan area, and genre you want. In return, you see all the radio stations that fit the description. (If you want to see all stations in a given city, select All Genres instead of a specific genre.)

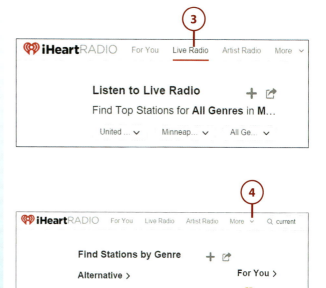

4 To listen to music of a particular type, click More and then click Genres. Select a genre from the list.

5 Once you click a station, you see that station's page. Click the Play button to start listening.

6 To stop (but not pause) playback, click the Stop button.

7 To add this station to your favorites, click the Options (three dots) button and then click Add to Favorites.

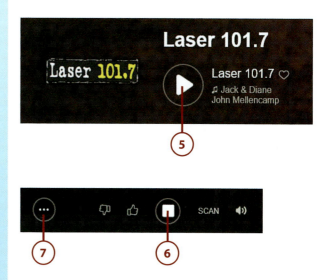

Listen to TuneIn

TuneIn is a competitor to iHeartRadio that streams live broadcasts from more than 100,000 radio stations around the world for free to any computer, smartphone, or tablet. You can find local stations from virtually every country around the world, which enables you to listen to the best music of any type, anywhere. You're not limited to primarily U.S. stations, nor to stations owned by a single media conglomerate.

To listen to TuneIn on your computer, point your web browser to www.tunein. com. (Mobile apps are also available for your smartphone or tablet.) You listen for free, although you probably want to establish an account (free) to keep track of your favorites.

1 Go to the TuneIn website (www.tunein.com) and sign up or sign in to your free account. TuneIn displays recommended stations, based on your past listening experience. Click a station to listen to it.

2 To search for a specific station, enter that station's call letters or city into the Search box and then press Enter.

3 To view all your local radio stations, click Local in the menu bar. You now see a list of local stations sorted by FM and then AM.

4 To find a specific station in a different city, click By Location and then drill down by continent, country, state (in the U.S.), and city.

5 To browse stations around the world by genre, click Music in the menu bar. Scroll down to the Explore section and then click through the genres until you find the station you want, wherever it happens to broadcast from.

6 When you select a station, you see that station's page, with the station's daily schedule and what's currently playing (if that info is available). If the station doesn't start playing automatically, click the Play button.

7 Click the Stop button to stop (not pause) playback.

8 Click the + to add this station to your favorites list.

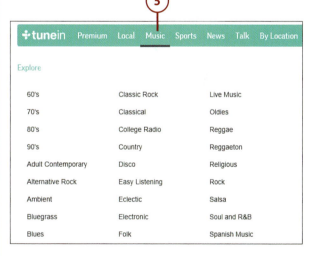

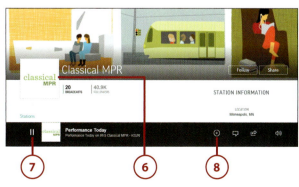

>>>Go Further

DOWNLOADING MUSIC FROM ONLINE MUSIC STORES

In addition to listening to streaming music services, you can also purchase and download digital music from a variety of online music stores. The music you purchase is downloaded to your computer or mobile device (phone or tablet) for listening at your convenience—even when you're not connected to the Internet.

The top three online music stores today are

- Amazon Digital Music Store (www.amazon.com/mp3/)

- Apple's iTunes Store (www.apple.com/itunes)

- Google Play Music (play.google.com/store/music)

All these online stores offer tens of millions of individual tracks and complete albums for purchase and download. Depending on the song and service, you pay between $0.69 and $1.29 per track; albums are in the $10+ range.

Microsoft Office Online

Google Docs Dashboard

In this chapter, you learn how to use cloud-based applications to do office work over the Internet.

- → Using Microsoft Office Online
- → Using Google Docs, Sheets, and Slides
- → Storing Your Files Online

11

Getting Productive Online

Go back a few years and if you wanted to use your computer to do word processing or spreadsheet work, you had to purchase and install an expensive piece of computer software, such as the Microsoft Office suite. Thanks to the Internet, however, you can now do your office work online, without purchasing or installing any software. It's all due to what we call *cloud computing* and web-based productivity apps that run over the Internet within any web browser.

The two most popular web-based productivity suites today are Microsoft Office Online and Google Docs. You use the individual apps in these suites to write letters and reports, do budgets and other number-crunching stuff, and create and give computer-based presentations. All you need is your computer, tablet, or smartphone, your favorite web browser, and a decent Internet connection. (And the best thing is—it's all free!)

Using Microsoft Office Online

Microsoft Office is the most popular software-based productivity suite and has been for almost two decades. You've probably used it yourself, or at least heard of it. You can, however, get most of the functionality of Microsoft Office for free, over the Internet, via Microsoft Office Online.

Microsoft Office Online is a web-based version of Microsoft Office that runs on any computer (and most tablets and smartphones) over the Internet. All you need to do is point your web browser to www.office.com, sign in to your Microsoft account, and then start working.

Office Online includes online versions of Microsoft's most popular applications. You'll find Word Online (word processing), Excel Online (spreadsheets), PowerPoint Online (presentations), OneNote Online (note taking), Outlook.com (email), and more.

Office Online Mobile

Microsoft offers Office Online apps for both Android and iOS devices. Functionality is more limited than with the web-based version, but it still lets you do basic editing and presenting from your smartphone or tablet. Search your device's app store to download the Word, Excel, and PowerPoint mobile apps.

It's Not All Good

Simpler—But More Limited

The individual apps in Microsoft Office Online are simpler and easier to use than the apps in the traditional software version of Microsoft Office. That's because they don't come with all the sophisticated functionality of the software programs. If you're not a power user, you can probably get by with the free online apps. However, if you do a lot of more sophisticated writing or number crunching, you may need to continue using the software-based version of Office instead.

Create or Open a File

You access Microsoft Office Online from within Google Chrome, Microsoft Edge, or any other web browser. Once you open the appropriate Office app, you can then create a new file or open an existing one.

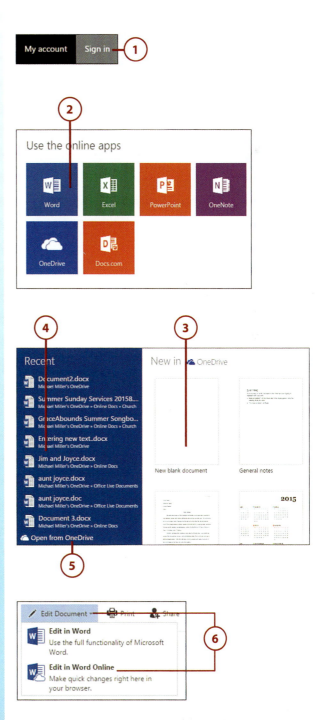

(1) Launch your web browser, go to www.office.com, and click Sign In to sign in to your Microsoft account. (If you don't yet have a Microsoft account, create one now; it's free.)

(2) On the next page, click the tile for the type of file you want to create.

(3) The home page for each app lists your most recently created files in the navigation pane on the left, as well as options on the right to create new files. Click a template to create a new document based on that template, or click New Blank Document to open a blank document.

(4) Click the name of a recent file to reopen that existing file.

(5) Click Open from OneDrive to open an older file.

(6) When the document opens, click Edit Document on the toolbar; then click Edit in *Application* Online.

Office Online from OneDrive

You can also open and edit existing documents from Microsoft OneDrive, which we discuss later in this chapter. Go to www.onedrive.com to view your online files; click a file to open it in the corresponding online app.

Use Word Online for Word Processing

When you want to write a letter, fire off a quick memo, create a report, or create a newsletter, you can use Microsoft Word Online. The Word Online workspace is similar to that of the software version, with a Ribbon at the top that provides all the buttons and controls you need to create and edit a document. Different tabs on the Ribbon display different collections of functions; click a tab, such as File, Home, Insert, or View, to access commands associated with that particular operation.

ScreenTips

If you're not sure just what a button on the Ribbon does, you're not alone—those little graphics are sometimes difficult to decipher. To display the name of any specific button, just hover your cursor over the button until the descriptive *ScreenTip* appears.

(1) Begin typing at the cursor to enter text into the document.

(2) Select a word, sentence, or paragraph by holding down your mouse button and dragging the cursor over the text you want to select. (You also can select text using your keyboard; use the Shift key—in combination with the arrow keys—to highlight blocks of text.) Any text you select appears with a gray highlight.

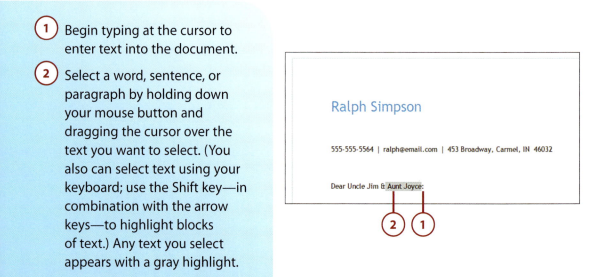

3 On the Home tab of the Ribbon, click Cut (or press Ctrl+X) to cut the selected text and prepare to move it to another location.

4 Click Copy on the Ribbon (or press Ctrl+C) to copy the selected text and prepare to paste it into another location.

5 Move the cursor to where you want to move or copy the selected text and then click Paste on the Ribbon (or press Ctrl+V).

6 Click any option in the Font section of the Ribbon's Home tab to format the selected text.

7 Click any option in the Paragraph section of the Ribbon's Home tab to format the current paragraph.

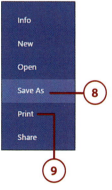

Deleting Text

To delete selected text, just press the Delete key on your computer keyboard.

8 To save your document with a new name, click the File tab on the Ribbon and then click Save As.

9 To print your document, click the File tab on the Ribbon and then click Print.

Use Excel Online for Spreadsheets

When you need to do a little number crunching, use Excel Online—the web-based version of the Microsoft Excel program.

>>>Go Further
UNDERSTANDING SPREADSHEETS

A spreadsheet is nothing more than a giant list. Your list can contain just about any type of data you can think of—text, numbers, and even dates. You can take any of the numbers on your list and use them to calculate new numbers. You can sort the items on your list, pretty them up, and print the important points in a report. You can even graph your numbers in a pie, line, or bar chart!

In a spreadsheet, everything is stored in little boxes called *cells*. Your spreadsheet is divided into many cells, each located in a specific location on a giant grid made of *rows* and *columns*. Each cell represents the intersection of a particular row and column, and is labeled as such. (For example, the cell at the intersection of column A and row 1 is labeled A1.)

1 To enter data into a cell, select the cell with your mouse or keyboard, type your text or numbers, and then press Enter.

2 To edit existing data in a cell, select the cell with your mouse or keyboard and make the edits in the Formula bar above the spreadsheet. Press Enter when done.

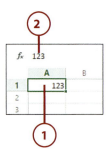

Formula Bar

You can also enter data directly into the Formula bar at the top of the spreadsheet. The Formula bar echoes the contents of the active cell.

3 To format the contents of a cell, select one or more cells; then select the appropriate option from the Font, Alignment, or Number sections of the Ribbon's Home tab.

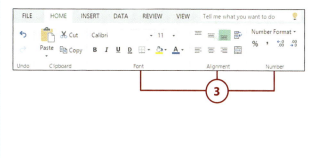

4 To enter a formula into a cell, select the cell, enter =, and then enter the formula. The formula can reference other cells and use the addition (+), subtraction (–), multiplication (*), and division (/) operators. So, for example, if you want to multiply 10 by 5, enter **=10*5**. If you want to divide the contents of cell A1 by the contents of cell A2, enter **=A1/A2**.

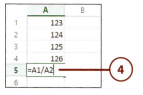

5 To create a chart from numeric data, select the range of cells you want to include and then select the Insert tab on the Ribbon. In the Charts section of the Insert tab, click the button for the type of chart you want to create. Excel displays a variety of charts within that general category; select the type of chart you want.

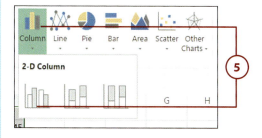

(6) To save your spreadsheet with a new name, click the File tab on the Ribbon and then click Save As.

(7) To print your spreadsheet, click the File tab on the Ribbon and then click Print.

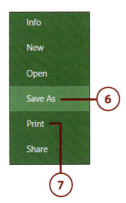

>>>Go Further

FUNCTIONS

In addition to the basic algebraic operators previously discussed, Excel includes a variety of *functions* that replace the complex steps present in many formulas. A function is essentially a prebuilt formula; all you have to do is enter the function and then insert the *arguments* (typically numbers or cell references) to complete the formula.

To enter a function, select a given cell, select the Home tab on the Ribbon, click the down arrow beneath the AutoSum button, and select More Functions. When the Insert Function dialog box appears, pull down the Select a Category list to display the functions of a particular type. Click the function you want to insert, click OK, and then enter the necessary arguments for that function. Click Enter when done.

Use PowerPoint Online for Presentations

When you need to present information to a group of people, the hip way to do it is with a PowerPoint presentation. You can use PowerPoint Online to create, edit, and give your presentations.

When you create a new presentation, PowerPoint starts with a single slide—the *title slide*. Naturally, you need to insert additional slides to create a complete presentation. PowerPoint lets you insert different types of slides, with different types of layouts for different types of information.

1. To insert a new slide, select the Home tab on the Ribbon and click the New Slide button. This displays the New Slide dialog box.

2. Select the slide layout you want and then click the Add Slide button.

3. To enter text into a slide, click the placeholder text and then enter your own words and numbers.

4. To format text on a slide, select the text you want to format and then click the appropriate button in the Font section of the Home tab.

Transitions and Animations

You can add transitions between slides and animate objects on a slide. Use the Transitions tab on the Ribbon to apply transitions and the Animations tab to apply animation effects.

5 To change the look and feel of the entire presentation, select the Design tab on the Ribbon and then choose a new theme from the Themes section.

6 To give a presentation, select the View tab and click the Slide Show button. To move from one slide to the next, all you have to do is click your mouse.

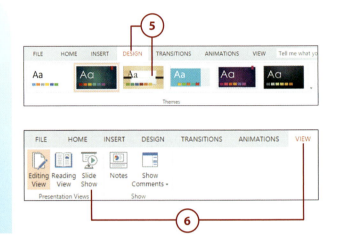

Using Google Docs, Sheets, and Slides

Google also offers a web-based suite of productivity applications. Google's apps are called Docs (word processing), Sheets (spreadsheet), and Slides (presentation). These web-based apps offer much the same functionality as the Office Online apps.

As with Office Online, Google Docs, Sheets, and Slides are completely free and run on any computer or mobile device in any web browser. All you need is an Internet connection (and a Google account, of course), and you're good to go.

Create or Open a File

You access Google's applications from within Microsoft Edge, Google Chrome, or any other web browser. Once you open the appropriate Google app, you can then create a new file or open an existing one.

1 Launch your web browser, go to docs.google.com, enter your password, and click Sign In to sign in to your Google account. (If you don't yet have a Google account, create one now; it's free.)

2 You now see a dashboard to all your online documents, with your word processing (Docs) documents front and center. To switch to documents from another app, click the Menu (three bar) button at the top left and select either Sheets or Slides.

3 To open an existing document, click its filename or thumbnail.

4 To create a new document, click a template or the + Blank thumbnail.

5 Google automatically saves each new document you create and when you make changes to that document. You can, however, give a new document a name, by clicking the Untitled box at the top of the page and entering a new name.

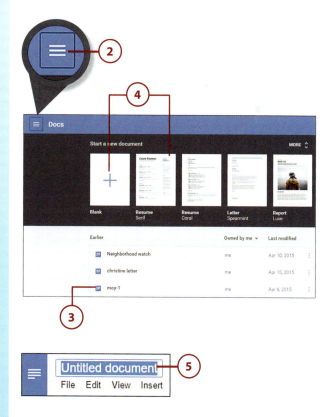

Use Google Docs for Word Processing

Google Docs is the word processing app in the Google suite. It works pretty much like Microsoft Word, and you use it for similar tasks—creating memos, letters, newsletters, and the like.

(1) Begin typing at the cursor to enter text into the document.

(2) Select a word, sentence, or paragraph by holding down your mouse button and dragging the cursor over the text you want to select. (You also can select text using your keyboard; use the Shift key—in combination with the arrow keys—to highlight blocks of text.) Any text you select appears with a light blue highlight.

(3) Click Edit, Cut (or press Ctrl+X) to cut the selected text and prepare to move it to another location.

(4) Click Edit, Copy (or press Ctrl+C) to copy the selected text and prepare to paste it into another location.

(5) Move the cursor to where you want to move or copy the selected text; then click Edit, Paste (or press Ctrl+V).

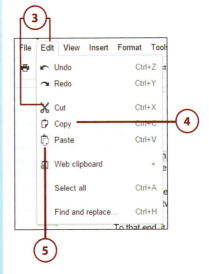

(2)

At this point in time, the best way to evaluate the issue is to look at visual representations. As you can see, there are several ways to approach the topic.

It was a peaceful day in the neighborhood. Only a select few were aware of the growing tensions between the two sides.

(1)

(3)

File	Edit	View	Insert	Format	Tool
	Undo			Ctrl+Z	
	Redo			Ctrl+Y	
	Cut			Ctrl+X	
	Copy			Ctrl+C	**(4)**
	Paste			Ctrl+V	
	Web clipboard			▸	
	Select all			Ctrl+A	
	Find and replace...			Ctrl+H	

(5)

Deleting Text

To delete selected text, just press the Delete key on your computer keyboard.

6 Click any option on the toolbar or on the Format menu to format the selected text or current paragraph.

7 To print your document, click File, Print.

Use Google Sheets for Spreadsheets

Google Sheets is the spreadsheet app in the Google suite. It offers most of the features and functionality found in Microsoft Excel, including charts, formulas, and a full complement of functions.

1 To enter data into a cell, select the cell with your mouse or keyboard, type your text or numbers, and then press Enter.

2 To edit existing data in a cell, select the cell with your mouse or keyboard and make the edits in the Formula bar above the spreadsheet. Press Enter when done.

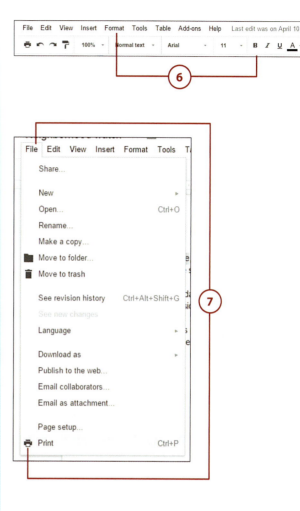

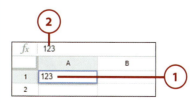

③ To format the contents of a cell, select one or more cells; then select the appropriate option on the toolbar or from the Format menu.

④ To enter a formula into a cell, select the cell, enter =, and then enter the formula. The formula can reference other cells and use the addition (+), subtraction (–), multiplication (*), and division (/) operators.

⑤ To enter a function, select the cell, click the Function button on the toolbar, and then select one of the listed functions or click More Functions to view all available functions.

⑥ To create a chart from numeric data, select the range of cells you want to include and then click Insert, Chart. When the Chart Editor appears, select the type of chart you want to create, as well as other available options; then click the Insert button.

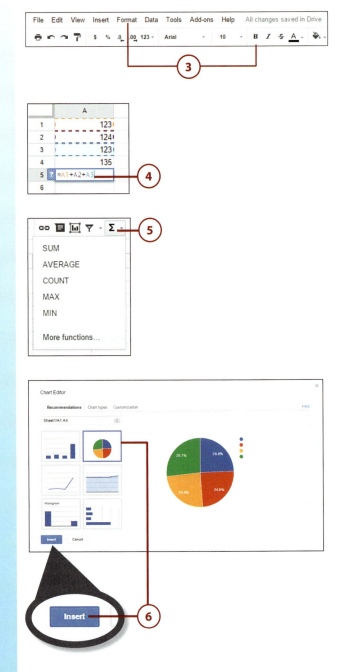

7 To print your spreadsheet, click File, Print.

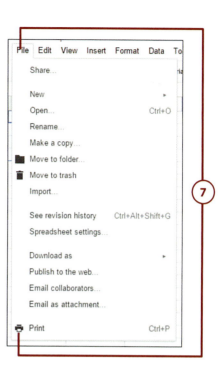

Use Google Slides for Presentations

Google Slides is the presentation app in the Google suite. It compares with PowerPoint in its capability to create and give professional-looking presentations.

1 To insert a new slide, select the down arrow next to the New Slide button; then select the desired layout.

2 To enter text into a slide, click the placeholder text and then enter your own words and numbers.

3 To format text on a slide, select the text you want to format and then click the appropriate option on the toolbar or on the Format menu.

4 To change the look and feel of the entire presentation, select Slide, Change Theme to display the Themes sidebar on the right side of the window. Click to select a new theme.

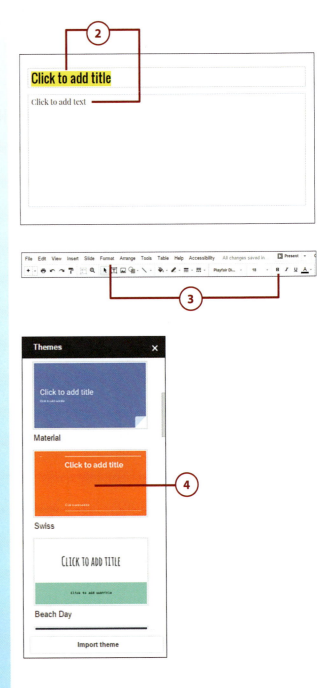

5 To apply a transition between slides, click Slide, Change Transition to display the Animations sidebar on the right side of the window. Click the Transition list to select a new transition.

6 To give a presentation, select the Present button at the top of the window. To move from one slide to the next, all you have to do is click your mouse.

Storing Your Files Online

Both Microsoft Office Online and Google Docs, Sheets, and Slides utilize *cloud storage* for the files you create. With cloud storage, files are stored online, not on your computer. You can then access these files—and allow others access—over the Internet, using any web browser.

Google's cloud-based storage service is called Google Drive. Microsoft's is called OneDrive. Both offer a fair amount of storage for free. Both also let you purchase additional storage for a fee.

Cloud Storage

Cloud storage is so named because the files are stored on the "cloud" of computers on the Internet. The primary advantage of cloud storage is that you can access files from any computer (work, home, or other) at any location; you're not limited to using a given file on one particular computer. You can also share web-based files with other users, to just view or to fully edit.

Use Google Drive

You view and manage your Google Drive files from the Drive website at drive.google.com.

1. Launch your web browser, go to drive.google.com, and (if necessary) sign in to your account.

2. The Google Drive website displays the files you've uploaded. If you've organized your files into folders, you see those folders on the main page. Click a folder to view its contents.

3. Click a file to view it or, in the case of a Docs, Sheets, or Slides file, open it in its host application.

4. To download a file from OneDrive to your local hard disk, select the file, click the More Actions (three dot) button, and then click Download.

5. To upload a file from your computer to Google Drive, click the New button and then select File Upload; when the Open dialog box appears, select the file to upload and then click Open.

Use Microsoft OneDrive

You view and manage your OneDrive files from the OneDrive website at onedrive.live.com.

1 Launch your web browser, go to onedrive.live.com, and (if necessary) sign in to your account.

2 The OneDrive website displays the files you've uploaded. If you've organized your files into folders, you see those folders on the main page. Click a folder to view its contents.

3 Click a file to view it or, in the case of an Office document, open it in its host application.

4 To download a file from OneDrive to your local hard disk, select the file and then click Download from the toolbar.

5 To upload a file from your computer to OneDrive, click Upload and then select Files; when the Open dialog box appears, select the file to upload; then click Open.

>>>Go Further

COMPARING ONLINE STORAGE SERVICES

Google Drive and Microsoft OneDrive are just two of many cloud storage services you can use to store and share your files online. The following table compares the features and pricing of some of the most popular services.

Online Storage Services

Service	URL	Free Storage	Other Plans
Apple iCloud	www.icloud.com	5GB	50GB $0.99/month 200GB $2.99/month 1TB $9.99/month
Box	www.box.com	10GB	100GB $5/month
Dropbox	www.dropbox.com	2GB	1TB $9.99/month
Google Drive	www.google.com/drive	15GB	100GB $1.99/month 1TB $9.99/month
Microsoft OneDrive	onedrive.live.com	5GB	50GB $1.99/month

All these services work similarly. Some, such as Google Drive, are better focused on collaboration and sharing. Check out the various services before you commit—especially for a paid plan.

Google Photos

Flickr

Sharing Your Photos Online

If you're like me, you use your smartphone or digital camera to take a lot of pictures. My wife and I happen to take a ton of photos of our grandkids (and you might do the same with your own children or grandchildren); other folks snap a lot of vacation photos, scenic shots, or just candid photos of people they know.

How do you share all these photos with your friends and family? In the old days, you'd head down to the drugstore or Fotomat, drop off your roll of film (that brings back memories!), and wait a week or so for your prints to be developed. Well, you can still get photo prints at your local drugstore (no more Fotomats, sorry), but it's a lot faster and easier to upload your photos to an online photo sharing service and let your friends and family view them over the Internet on their own computers, tablets, and smartphones. It's easy to do, a lot more convenient than making photo prints, and (in most cases) completely free.

There are many photo sharing sites out there on the Web. They all work pretty much the same way. You upload your digital photos from your computer or phone or whatever to the photo sharing site, and then (if you like) organize them into virtual photo albums or folders. You select the photo or album or folder you want to share, and then send the web address for that item to hopefully interested friends and family. When someone clicks the link you send, she sees the photos you decided to share. She can then view the photos, download them to her own computer, and print them on her printer.

This chapter covers three popular photo sharing sites that focus on three different types of users and uses. Google Photo is a great site for casual users who want to share photos not only with other users but also between their own smartphones, tablets, and computers. Flickr is a site for more serious hobbyist and professional photographers, with sophisticated features that appeal to that audience. And Shutterfly is a commercial site that makes it easy to create prints of your favorite photos. Read on to learn more.

Sharing Photos with Google Photos

Google Photos (photos.google.com) is one of the most versatile and popular photo sharing sites for everyday users. You can use Google Photos to share your pictures with others, to store your photos (and free up disk space on your computer or mobile device), or just to back up the photos you store elsewhere. Google Photos is completely free (all you need is an equally free Google account), and you can store an unlimited number of photos online. That's right, unlimited photo storage for free. What's not to like?

It's Not All Good

Unlimited—With Limits

While it's true that Google Photos lets you store an unlimited number of photos, that's only if you store them at a reduced resolution. Now, that reduced resolution is pretty good—16 megapixels—but that may be lower quality than your originals.

If you opt to store your photos at their original resolution, you're limited to just 15GB of storage space. You can buy additional storage, of course; an extra 100GB runs $1.99/month, or you can purchase 1TB extra for $9.99/month.

Storing your photos at their original resolution may make sense if you're a professional or serious hobbyist photographer. For most everyday users, 16 megapixel resolution is just fine, thank you, and gets you the free unlimited storage. (Google automatically resizes your photos if you upload photos over the 16MP limit.)

To switch from unlimited storage at what Google calls "high quality" to the more limited original resolution storage, click the Settings (three bar) icon at the top-left corner of the page and then select Settings. On the next page, select either High Quality (Free Unlimited Storage) or Original. You can change from one plan to another at any time.

Upload Photos from Your PC

If you have a bunch of photos on your computer you want to store with Google Photos, you have to upload them to the Google Photos site. You do this by pointing any web browser to the Google Photos site, located at photos.google.com. (If you haven't yet signed in to your Google account, do so now—or create a new account if you don't yet have one.)

1. From the main page, click the Upload Photos (cloud) icon to display the Open dialog box.

2. Navigate to and select the photos you want to upload. (To select multiple photos, press and hold the Ctrl key while clicking each photo.)

3. Click the Open button. The photos are now uploaded and you see the confirmation dialog box.

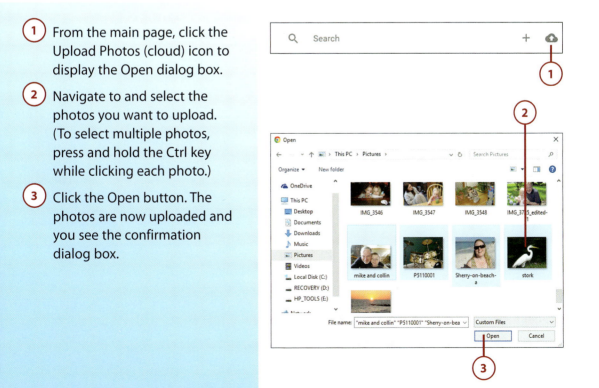

4 To add these photos to an existing photo album, click Add to Album and then select an album.

5 To create a new photo album for these photos, click Create Album to display a new album page; then enter a name for this new album.

6 To view these photos online, click View Photos.

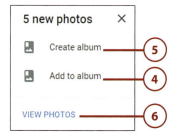

Videos

Google Photos also lets you upload and share videos.

View Photos

You can view your Google Photos pictures in two different ways. First, you can simply view them in chronological order. Second, you can view them in photo albums or collections. (A collection is a photo album that Google creates for you.)

1 Click the Photos icon to display photos in reverse chronological order—newest first, grouped by date.

2 Click the Collections icon to display photos by album or collection.

3 Click an album or collection to view all photos within.

(**4**) Click a photo to view it larger in your browser window.

(**5**) Click Zoom In to make the picture bigger. Click the resulting Zoom Out icon to return the picture to the original size.

(**6**) Click Open Info to view more information about this photo.

(**7**) Mouse over the photo and click the right or left arrows to move to the next or previous photo. (You can also press the left and right arrow keys on your computer keyboard.)

(**8**) Click the back arrow at the top left to return to the album, collection, or photos by date.

Share Photos with Others

Google Photos offers several ways to share a photo with others. You can share it via email (by including a link to the photo in an email message), or via Facebook, Twitter, or Google+ (Google's social network).

(**1**) Open the album, collection, or photo you want to share; then click the Share icon at the top of the photo.

2 To share via Facebook or another social network, click the appropriate icon to display a new message window for that network.

3 Enter a message to accompany the selected item.

4 Click the Post button.

5 To share via email, click Get Shareable Link.

6 Right-click the resulting link and select Copy.

7 Open a new email message in your email program or service.

8 Position the cursor within the body of the message; then right-click and select Paste. This inserts a link to the photo into the email message.

9 Complete and send the message as normal.

Share ✕

https://goo.gl/photos/iWNzNxeLNU5p — **6**

Delete

7   **8**

New Message   – ⤢ ✕

Recipients

Subject

Undo	Ctrl+Z
Redo	Ctrl+Shift+Z
Cut	Ctrl+X
Copy	Ctrl+C
Paste	**Ctrl+V**
Paste as plain text	Ctrl+Shift+V
Delete	
Spell-checker options	▸
Writing Direction	▸
Select all	Ctrl+A
Inspect element	Ctrl+Shift+I

Sans Serif

Send

9

Download Photos to Your PC

Anyone with a link to a photo, collection, or album can download the referenced photos to his own computer. From there, he can print the photo on his printer or even send the photo to a photo printing service to make professional prints.

1 Open the album, collection, or photo you want to download; then click the More (three dot) icon at the top of the photo.

2 Select either Download (for an individual photo) or Download All (for an album or collection).

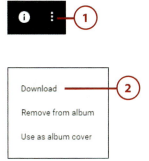

Download ——— **2**

Remove from album

Use as album cover

③ Depending on your web browser, the photos may be automatically saved to a default location or you may be prompted to choose a location. If you see a Save As dialog box, navigate to where you want to download the photo(s) and then click Save.

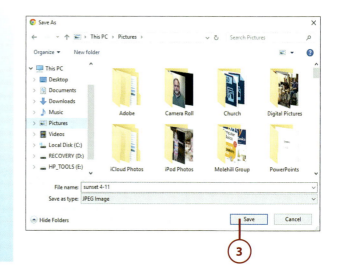

Use the Google Photos Mobile App

If you install the Google Photos app on your smartphone or tablet, any photo you shoot is uploaded to Google Photos. You don't have to do a thing; the photos you shoot are automatically backed up online.

Android and iOS

The Google Photos mobile app is available for both Android and iOS devices and is free for download in your device's app store. Both Android and iOS versions work similarly; we use the Android app for the examples in this section.

1 Open the Google Photos app and scroll through the available photos in reverse chronological order.

2 To view photos by album or collection, tap the Menu (three line) icon and select Collections.

3 Tap to open the desired album or collection.

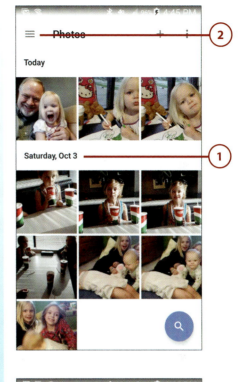

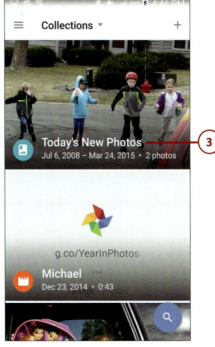

4 Tap a picture to view it full screen.

5 To edit a photo, tap the Edit (pencil icon) and then select an editing option—Auto, Light, Color, Pop, Vignette, or Crop.

6 To view more information about a photo, tap the Info icon.

7 To share a picture, tap the Share icon to display the Sharing pane.

8 Tap how you want to share the photo—via Facebook or other social media, email, instant message, and so forth.

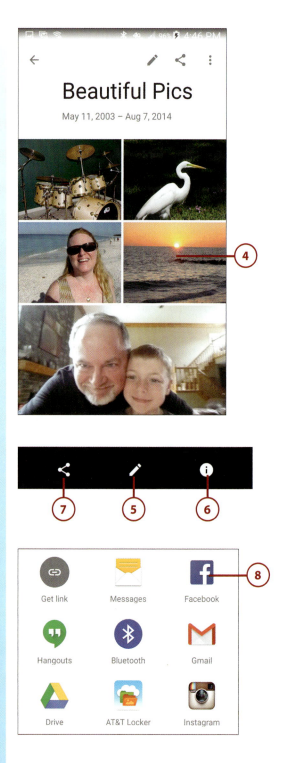

Sharing Photos on Flickr

Flickr (www.flickr.com) is the photo sharing service preferred by serious photographers. Photos are uploaded to and stored on Flicker in their full original resolution, although others can download photos at a variety of resolutions.

Yahoo!

Flickr is owned by Yahoo! You can log on to Flickr with a dedicated Flickr account or with your Yahoo! account, if you have one.

Flickr offers three types of accounts. The basic Free account is, naturally, free, and lets you store up to 1TB of photos and videos. The Ad Free option offers the same storage capability but doesn't display ads on pages; it runs $5.99/month or $49.99/year. The Doublr account offers 2TB of storage for $499/year. For most of us, the Free account is just fine. (For all practical purposes, 1TB of storage will hold well over a million average-sized digital photos.)

Upload Photos from Your PC

Uploading photos from your computer to Flickr is easy to do from within any web browser.

1. From the Flicker home page (www.flickr.com), click the Upload icon to display the Upload page.

2. Click Choose Photos and Videos to display the Open dialog box.

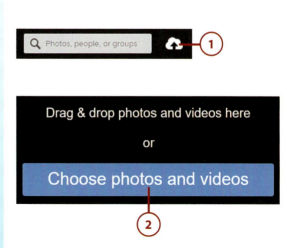

(3) Navigate to and select the photo(s) you want to upload. (Hold down the Ctrl key to select multiple photos.)

(4) Click the Open button. This displays the photo(s) you selected.

(5) Click the name of the photo to edit or change the name.

(6) Click Add a Description to add a description to this photo.

(7) Click Add Tags to tag this photo with descriptive keywords.

(8) Click Add to Albums to add this photo to one or more photo albums.

(9) Click the Upload button to upload this and other photos.

View Photos

Flickr displays your photos in a number of ways. You can view your Photostream, which displays all the photos you've uploaded, newest first. You can view your Camera Roll, which is like the Photostream except with photos grouped by date. And you can display photos in Albums that you create.

(**1**) The Flickr home page displays photos from other users you follow. To view your own photos, click You in the menu bar.

(**2**) Click Camera Roll to view pictures sorted by date, with newest pictures first.

(**3**) Click Photostream to view pictures by date, newest first.

(**4**) Click Albums to view your photo albums.

(**5**) Click a photo album to view all photos within.

(**6**) Click a photo to view it larger.

7 Click the Expand icon to view a photo in the full browser window. (Click Expand again to return to the normal view.)

8 Click the right or left arrows to move to the next or previous photo. (You can also press the right or left arrow keys on your computer keyboard.)

9 Click Back to Album to return to the photo album, or Back to Photostream to return to the Photostream.

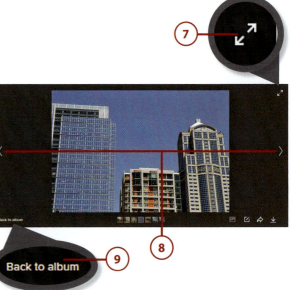

Download Photos to Your PC

Flickr lets you download photos at a variety of popular resolutions and sizes—square, small, medium, large, and original (full resolution).

1 Click to open the photo you want to download; then click the Download icon.

2 Select the desired size/ resolution to begin the download.

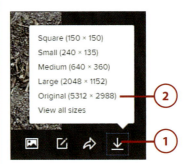

③ With some web browsers, the photo will be automatically downloaded to a default location on your system. With other browsers, you may be prompted to choose a download location. If you see the Save As dialog box, navigate to the location where you want to download the photo and then click the Save button.

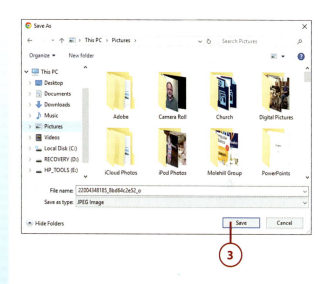

Share Photos with Others

Flickr lets you share photos with others via Facebook, Pinterest, Tumblr, Twitter, and email.

① Click to open the photo you want to share; then click the Share icon.

② Click how you want to share this photo and then follow the onscreen instructions to share the photo.

3. To share on Facebook, enter an optional message; then click Post to Facebook.

4. To share on Pinterest, enter or edit the description and choose the desired board to pin to.

5. To share via email, enter the recipient's email address and an accompanying message; then click Share.

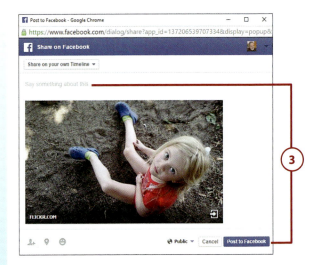

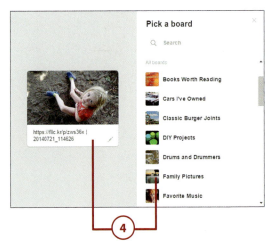

Sharing Photos on Shutterfly

In addition to free services such as Google Photos and Flickr, there are many commercial photo sharing/printing sites online that exist primarily to create prints of your photos—for a price. One of the most popular of these services is Shutterfly—although they all offer similar services at similar pricing.

Let's be straight about this. Unlike Google Photos and Flickr, Shutterfly and similar sites are commercial services out to make money by selling you stuff. Primarily, they sell prints of your photos, although they also offer a variety of other products, from photo calendars to coffee mugs to tee shirts. When you create a Shutterfly account (which is free), you get free unlimited photo storage; Shutterfly hopes that, over time, you'll spend enough money on printed products to make it all worthwhile.

Upload Photos from Your PC

Before you can do anything on Shutterfly, you need to upload your photos, which you do from any web browser. Just go to www.shutterfly. com and create or sign in to your account.

1. From the Shutterfly home page, click My Pictures.

2. Click the Upload button to display the Upload Pictures window.

3. Click the Choose Files button to display the Open dialog box.

4. Navigate to and select the photos you want to upload. (Press and hold the Ctrl key to select multiple photos.)

5. Click the Open button.

6. To upload to a new photo album, check Create New Album and enter a name for the album.

7. To upload to an existing photo album, check Upload to Existing Album and then select the album from the list.

8. Click the Start button.

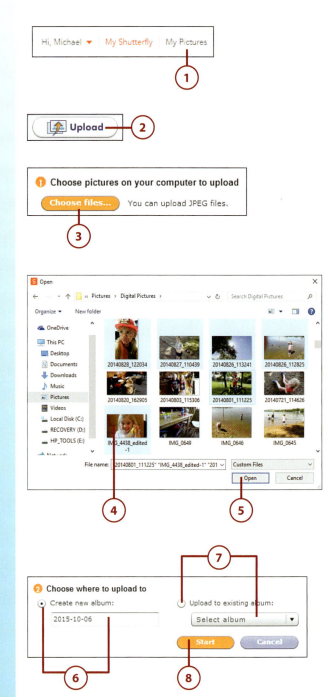

9 When the upload is completed you see the Upload Completed page. Click View Pictures to view the uploaded photos.

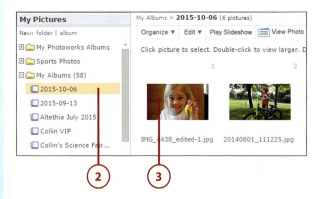

View Your Photos

The photos you upload are stored in the My Pictures part of the Shutterfly site.

1 From the Shutterfly home page, click My Pictures.

2 In the My Pictures sidebar on the left, click to select a photo album. This displays all the photos in that album.

3 Double-click a thumbnail to display a larger version of that picture.

4 Click the right and left arrows to move to the next or previous picture.

5 Click a thumbnail beneath this picture to go directly to another photo in this album.

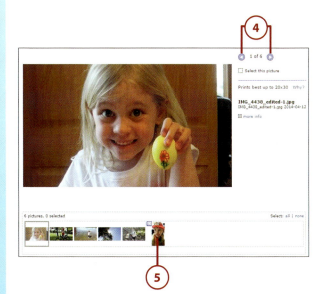

Share Photos with Others

Shutterfly lets you share photo albums or individual photos via email.

Share Sites

Shutterfly also lets you create what it calls Share sites. A Share site is a website, hosted on the Shutterfly site, that displays selected photos that you share publicly with others. Share sites are great for photos of group events and organizations, such as softball teams, bowling leagues, book clubs, and the like.

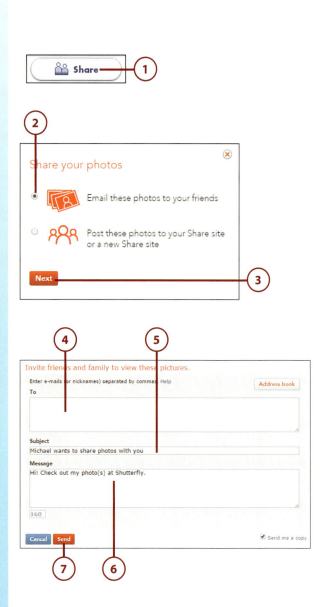

1. Open the photo album or photo you want to share and then click the Share button to display the Share Your Photos panel.

2. Click to select Email These Photos to Your Friends.

3. Click Next.

4. Enter the recipient's email address into the To box. To send to multiple recipients, separate email addresses with commas.

5. Accept or edit the Subject line.

6. Accept or enter your own message in the Message box.

7. Click the Send button.

Print Photos

Shutterfly is in the business of selling photo prints. You can order prints directly from Shutterfly, which are then mailed to you in a few days, or you can order prints to be picked up at your local CVS, Target, or Walgreens store. Local pickup is only available for 4 x 6 glossy prints with no printing on the back and are typically available for pickup in about an hour.

(1) Navigate to and select the photo(s) you want to print.

(2) Click the Order Prints button to display the Prints page.

(3) In the Picture section, select how many of which size print you want for each photo selected.

(4) By default, Shutterfly prints the file name and date on the back of each photo. Since you can't get local pickup for photos with this printing on the back, delete the message text and click Apply This Message to All Prints.

(5) Click the Next button.

(6) On the next page, confirm the information and click the Continue to Cart button.

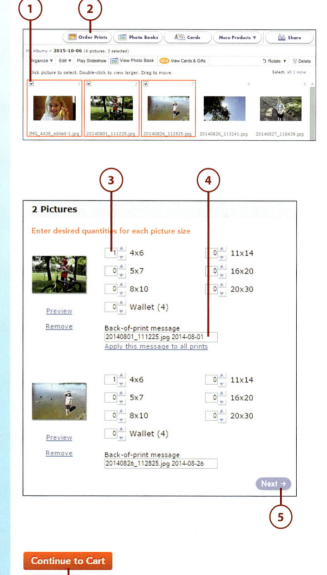

7 On the Shopping Cart page, confirm your order and then click the Checkout button to display the Your Order page.

8 To pick up these prints locally, click 1-Hour Pick Up Available and continue through to choose the pickup location.

9 To have these prints shipped to you, enter or confirm your shipping information.

10 Choose a delivery option.

11 Enter or edit your payment information.

12 Click the Order button to place your order.

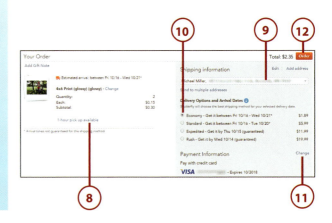

>>>*Go Further*
SHARING PHOTOS ON FACEBOOK

Many people do their photo sharing via social media, especially on Facebook. Not only can you post individual photos as part of your status updates, Facebook also lets you create photo albums that all your online friends can view.

To create a photo album on Facebook, click your name in the toolbar to display your Timeline page. Click Photos to display all your current photos; then click Create Album. Select the photos to upload, enter a name for the album, and your photos are now online for all your Facebook friends to see.

Ancestry.com

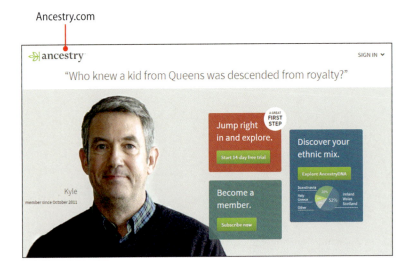

FamilySearch

In this chapter, you learn how to find out more about your family history at genealogy websites.

→ Using Ancestry.com
→ Using FamilySearch

13

Exploring Your Genealogy Online

As the years continue to pass, many of us get more interested in our family history. Genealogy is the study of families and lineages, and it's a big deal online. There are many sites you can use to find long-lost relatives and fill in your family tree.

Using Ancestry.com

Ancestry.com (www.ancestry.com) is the most popular genealogy site on the Web and a great place to start researching your family history. It's a paid site (with a 14-day free trial), but there's a ton of information to be found here.

The company behind Ancestry.com operates a network of genealogy and historical record websites. It manages more than 16 billion online records and has more than 2 million subscribers—who themselves have uploaded close to 200 million photos and created more than 70 million family trees.

Subscriptions

Ancestry.com offers several different types of subscriptions. U.S. Discovery (access to all U.S. records) runs $19.99/month or $99 for six months. World Explorer (access to all U.S. and international records) runs $34.99/month or $149 for six months. All Access adds access to other related sites for $44.99/month or $199 for six months.

Start Your Family Tree

The best place to get started with Ancestry.com is with your family tree. Enter as much information as you know about your mother, father, and other family members, and Ancestry.com starts filling in the branches.

1. Go to www.ancestry.com and either create a new account or sign in to an existing account.

2. On the menu bar, click Trees and then click Start a New Tree.

3. Click Add Yourself at the top (left side) of the tree.

4. Enter as much information about yourself as you can (name, gender, birthdate, and so forth) and then click Continue.

5 Click another person on the tree—your mother, father, or spouse.

6 Enter as much information as possible about this person; then click Save.

7 Click other people on the tree to add information about them.

8 Click Add Relative to add other relatives to the tree.

9 If the site has an ancestry hint about a person, it displays a green leaf. Click that person's name to display a detail panel.

10 Click Ancestry Hint(s) to display the hints.

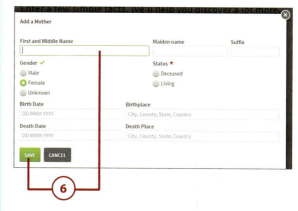

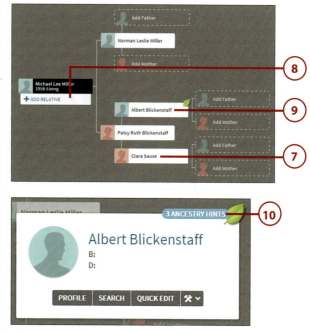

11 Click Review to look at any specific hint.

12 Select the information you want to review.

13 Click Review Selected Tree Hints.

14 Check the information you want to add to your family tree.

15 Click Save to Your Tree.

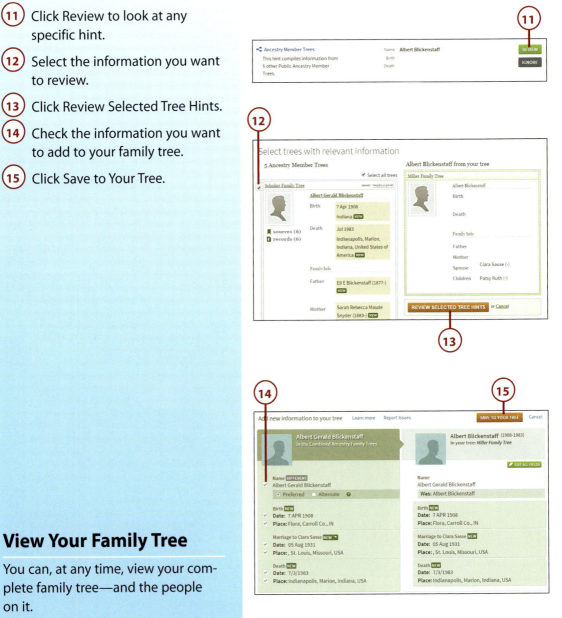

View Your Family Tree

You can, at any time, view your complete family tree—and the people on it.

1 From the menu bar, click Trees; then click the name of your family tree.

2 By default, you see the tree in what the site calls Pedigree view. To switch to a more traditional view of your family tree, click the Family View button.

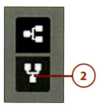

3 Drag the rectangle in the navigation box to view specific parts of your tree. (Alternatively, you can use your mouse to click and drag anywhere on the screen to move around the tree.)

4 Click a person to display an information pane for that individual.

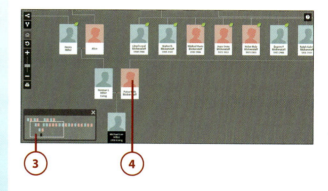

5 Click the Profile button to display that person's detailed profile page.

6 Click any piece of information to edit it.

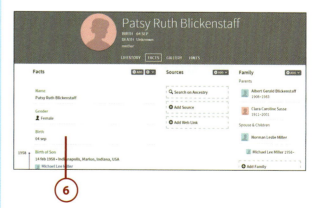

Using FamilySearch

FamilySearch (www.familysearch.org) is another useful site for amateur genealogists. The site searches millions of digitized records from sources worldwide.

To use FamilySearch, you need to create an account for yourself. Unlike Ancestry.com, FamilySearch is completely free.

Mormons

FamilySearch is owned and managed by the Church of Jesus Christ of Latter-Day Saints—Mormons, in other words. The LDS church places a high value on family history and keeps a large database of historical records, which are perfect for genealogical purposes.

Create a Family Tree

All genealogy starts with a family tree, which you can create easily on the FamilySearch site.

1. Go to www.familysearch.org and create a new account or sign in to an existing account.

2. In the menu bar, click Family Tree; then click Tree.

3 Click Add Husband or Add Wife to add your spouse.

4 Click Add Husband or Add Wife to add your parents.

5 Click Children; then click Add Child to add a child.

6 Enter as much information as you know about the new person.

7 Click Next.

8 The next pane tells you whether the person you added has a match in the FamilySearch database. Click either Add Match (if it's a match) or Add New (if it's not) to add this person to your family tree.

9 Keep clicking positions to add new people to your family tree.

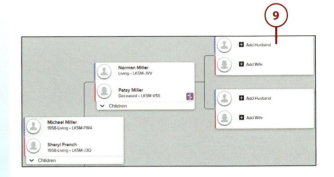

Search for Additional Information

FamilySearch lets you search a variety of historical records to find more information about specific family members.

1 From the menu bar, click Search; then click Records to display the Search Historical Records page.

2 Enter the person's first and last name into the First Names and Last Names boxes.

3 Enter any other pertinent information that might narrow your search.

4 Click the Search button to display the search results page.

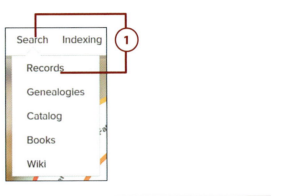

5 Click the Details icon to view more information about a given item.

6 Click Attach to Family Tree to add this information to your family tree.

Search Results from Historical Records

1-20 of 1,278 results for Name: **Albert Blickenstaff**

Number of results to show: 20 50 75

Attach to Family Tree — **6**

>>>Go Further

OTHER USEFUL GENEALOGY SITES

Many other sites are available online where you can find information about your family history. Check out the following:

- AfriGeneas (www.afrigeneas.com), a free site for researching African-American roots
- Cyndi's List (www.cyndislist.com), which offers a large list of genealogy-related websites
- Find A Grave (www.findagrave.com), part of the Ancestry.com family of sites, which helps you find grave records of family members, celebrities, and just about anybody you can think of
- Mocavo (www.mocavo.com), a free genealogy search engine for finding records and other relevant information across the Web.
- MyHeritage (www.myheritage.com), another free full-service genealogy and family tree site

In addition, there's no harm in using Google to search for specific people in your family. Just enter the person's full name and any other relevant information (where they live or lived, birthdate, and so forth) and let Google search the Web for you.

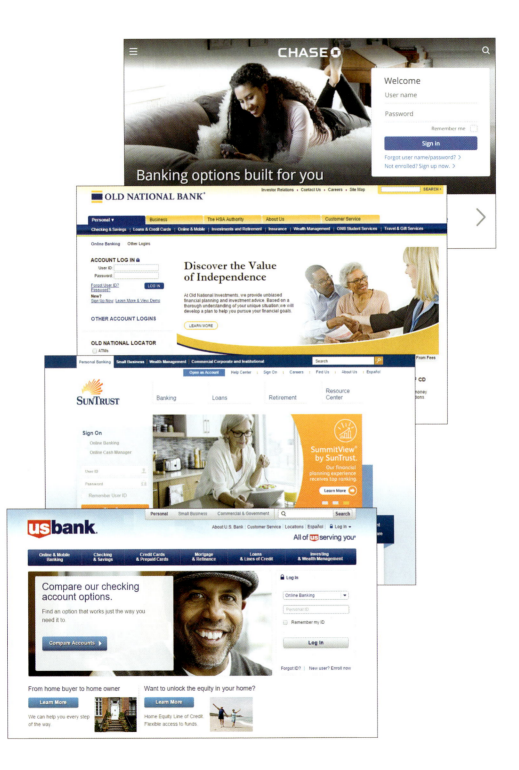

In this chapter, you learn how to do your banking and manage your finances over the Internet.

→ Banking Online
→ Tracking Your Investments

Managing Your Finances Online

The Internet makes it easy to do all sorts of financial transactions. No longer do you need to drive to the bank and stand in line to see a teller; just about everything you can do at the bank can now be done online. Same thing with paying bills; forget the stamps and envelopes and pay your bills electronically, via your web browser. You can even check the performance of your investments online. You never have to leave home!

Banking Online

Banking from the convenience of your own home, using your own computer (or tablet or smartphone) makes life a lot easier for all of us, especially those who have trouble getting around. Every morning I log in to my bank's website, check my balances, and make any necessary transfers. Once a week or so I pay bills online, typically through the individual websites of my utility companies, cable company, phone company, and the like. It takes just a few minutes and then I'm done— no driving involved!

Do Online Banking

Online banking might be new to you, but it's been around for more than a decade now. Almost all banks and credit unions have their own websites that let you view and reconcile your checking and savings accounts, transfer funds, and more.

To do your banking online, you need to set up an online account with your bank or financial institution. Consult your bank for details, but typically you need to enter your bank account numbers, personal identification numbers (PINs), and other personal data to create your account. After you create your account, all you need to do to log in is enter your username and password.

1 Most banks let you view your account balances online. Click an account to view your most recent transactions

2 Click a transaction to view more details—including, in some instances, scans of printed checks.

3 Many banks also let you transfer funds between accounts, such as between a checking and savings account.

Pay Your Bills Online

Many banks let you set up bill payments from their websites. In other instances, you can go directly to a payee's website and make your payments there. You typically pay via electronic transfer from your bank account—or, in some instances, via credit card. If you go this route you need to set up an online account before you pay.

(1) Most credit card sites let you view your most recent transactions.

(2) Most sites display a summary of your current account information.

(3) Click the "pay" link to enter payment information and pay your current bill.

(1)

Transaction Details for Period Ending 09/29/2015

Please note that if you made an Online Bill or Phone Payment between 5 p.m. ET and midnight ET on your statement Due Date, you will see a temporary late fee applied to your account. Once your payment has posted, the late fee will be removed.

Date ▼	Description ▼▲	Amount ▼▲
09/29/2015	INTEREST CHARGE ON CASH ADVANCES	0.00
09/29/2015	INTEREST CHARGE ON PURCHASES	9.76
09/25/2015	PAYMENT - THANK YOU	-160.00
09/19/2015	206 CR 42 APPLE VALLEY MN	31.42
09/19/2015	14301 NICOLLET CT BURNSVILLE MN	28.25
09/04/2015	206 CR 42 APPLE VALLEY MN	29.02
09/01/2015	PAYMENT - THANK YOU	-65.30

Print This Page

(2)

Current Balance	Minimum Payment Due	Payment Due Oct. 26, 2015
$416.72	**$25.00**	Make a Payment ▶ **(3)**
	• Minimum Payment Warning	

		Activity Since Last Statement		View/Update Card Options
Last Statement Balance - 09/29/2015	$386.45	Payments/Adjustments/Credits	$0.00	
Next Statement	Oct. 30, 2015	Purchases/Debits	$30.27	Special offers & services
Total Credit Limit	$550.00	Available for Purchase	$133.00	
Last Payment	Sep. 25, 2015	Available for Cash	$50.00	
Last Payment Amount	$160.00	• View/Edit Scheduled Payments		
Past Due Amount	$0.00			

It's Not All Good

Safety First

When you're dealing with websites that contain sensitive information, such as banks and other financial sites, make sure you sign out of the site when you're done using it. You don't want some other user of your computer to be able to access your personal information, just because you left the site open on your PC.

It's also a good idea to not do your online banking at public Wi-Fi hotspots. Public Wi-Fi isn't nearly as secure as your home wireless network, and you don't want electronic eavesdroppers stealing your private banking information. In other words, wait and do your online banking at home.

In addition, make sure you create a super secure password for all the banking and financial sites you use. Make sure it's long and complex and unguessable—and create different passwords for each site. You don't want strangers accessing your computer and getting into your bank accounts online.

Tracking Your Investments

Whether you have a small nest egg or a larger one, you can find a lot of information and services online to help you manage what money you have.

View Financial Information Online

If you have a number of investments—in stocks, mutual funds, IRAs, or 401(k) plans—you can track their performance online in real time. A number of websites offer both investment tracking and financial news and advice.

(1) CNN Money (money.cnn.com) is the online home of both *Fortune* and *Money* magazines. In addition to some of the best financial news and opinion on the Web, you can also use the site to create a watch list of your own personal investments and then track your investments over time.

(2) The Motley Fool (www.fool.com) has more opinion and advice than competing financial sites, and is both fun and useful. Plus, of course, you can create your own watch list to track your investments.

3 Yahoo! Finance (finance.yahoo.com) is the most popular financial website today. It's loaded with tons of financial news and opinion, and lets you track your own portfolio online.

3

>>>Go Further

MINT

If you want to manage all your financial transactions in one place, consider signing up for Mint. Mint is a personal finance site where you can enter all your online accounts (banking, credit cards—you name it) and view your daily activities online. You can use Mint to pay bills, transfer funds, and perform other essential tasks—as well as review your income and expenditures over time.

Unlike financial management software, such as Quicken (whose parent company owns Mint, believe it or not), Mint is totally free to use. Learn more at www.mint.com.

In this chapter, you learn how to use the Internet to manage your medical conditions— and stay healthy.

→ Finding Medical Information Online
→ Searching for Physicians Online
→ Ordering Prescription Drugs Online

Tracking Your Health Online

If you or one of your family members is sick, you want answers *now*. Whether you're dealing with the common cold, a nagging back pain, or something much more serious, there is no better or faster place to turn to than the numerous health-related sites on the Web. Online you get access to the same medical databases used by most physicians, and your access is immediate—no waiting for an appointment!

Finding Medical Information Online

Whether you need to research a particular medical condition, make a doctor's appointment, or fill a prescription, you can do it online. The Internet is indeed a great source of healthcare information and services for patients of any age.

Search Online Health Sites

Have a new ache or pain? Stubborn cough? Just not feeling right?

When you need information about what ails you, fire up your web browser and go online. While you can always do a simple Google search for today's symptoms, better and more specialized health-related sites are available. Turn to these websites to research all sorts of medical conditions before you call your doctor.

1 WebMD (www.webmd.com) is one of the most popular websites for researching all sorts of ailments and conditions. The site features sections for specific health conditions, drugs and supplements, and healthy living, along with a symptom checker and physician directory.

2 MedicineNet.com (www. medicinenet.com) features health news and information, including a huge database of diseases and conditions, pharmaceutical reference guide, medical dictionary, and online symptom checker.

3 The National Institutes of Health offers the SeniorHealth website (www.nihseniorhealth.gov), with stories, videos, and other information specifically geared toward a 50 and over audience.

>>>Go Further

OTHER ONLINE HEALTH SITES

MedicineNet.com, SeniorHealth, and WebMD are just a few of the many websites offering health-related information of interest to those of us aged 50 and over. The following sites may also be of interest:

- **AARP Health (www.aarp.org/health).** Health-related news and information for 50+ users, including information on healthy living, Medicare, drugs and supplements, and more.

- **About Health (www.about.com/health).** News and information about a broad range of healthcare topics. Click Senior Health in the left sidebar to access topics of interest to people aged 50 and over, such as Senior Care, Caregiving, Healthy Aging, and Menopause.

- **healthfinder (www.healthfinder.gov).** Links to a variety of health-related resources, from the U.S. Department of Health and Human Services.

- **HealthLinks.net (www.healthlinks.net).** A comprehensive directory to a variety of healthcare information.

- **MedExplorer (www.medexplorer.com).** Terrific directory and search engine for a variety of health and medical information.

- **Medicine Online (www.medicineonline.com).** Good site for general medical information. Also includes a physician search feature and a physician available 24/7 to answer health-related questions online.

- **Medscape (www.medscape.com).** Medical and health-related news and information.

- **Yahoo! Health (www.yahoo.com/health).** Health-related news and information.

These sites are superb resources for all sorts of medical information, particularly useful in diagnosing medical conditions and in encouraging preventive healthcare.

It's Not All Good

Trust Your Physician

The health information you find online is not always as accurate or relevant as that offered by your own personal physician. It's possible to get advice online that doesn't actually apply to your personal medical condition or that doesn't reflect the best approach to diagnosing or treating your condition. (It's also easy to misdiagnose yourself—especially if you tend to be a bit of a hypochondriac!) While you can get a lot of useful background information online, it's always best to consult with your physician in person to get the advice that's best for you.

Searching for Physicians Online

Looking for a new doctor? A number of websites let you search for a new or specialist physician or clinic near you. Some of these sites also let you look for other types of medical professionals.

Find a Doctor

Whether you're looking for a general practitioner or some sort of specialist, these websites can help you find the right doctor in your area.

1. Find a Doctor (www.findadoctor.com) lets you search for physicians by specialty and location, and then schedule an appointment—all online.

2. The American Medical Association maintains a comprehensive database on more than 814,000 licensed doctors nationwide. The AMA's DoctorFinder site (apps.ama-assn.org/doctorfinder/) lets you search this database for a doctor near you.

3. When you're looking for physicians and healthcare professionals who are enrolled in the Medicare program, use Medicare's official Physician Compare site (www.medicare.gov/physiciancompare/).

>>>*Go Further*

PHYSICIAN SEARCHES

There are even more sites that let you search for physicians online. The most popular include the following:

- 1-800-DOCTORS.com (www.1-800-doctors.com)
- DoctorDirectory.com (www.doctordirectory.com)
- healthgrades (www.healthgrades.com)
- WebMD Physician Directory (doctor.webmd.com)
- ZocDoc (www.zocdoc.com)

In addition, many physicians, medical groups, clinics, and hospitals have their own sites on the Web. Some of these sites are informational only, but a growing number let you schedule appointments or review your medical records from the convenience of your web browser.

Ordering Prescription Drugs Online

Hand in hand with online doctors come online pharmacists. Make no mistake about it—online drugstores are a big business and convenient for their customers.

Most online drugstores work just like real-world drugstores, except with FedEx thrown in for the legwork: They receive your prescription, they fill it, and then they ship it to you. Just like that—no fuss, no muss.

In fact, some of the online sites *are* real-world drugstores; CVS, Rite Aid, and Walgreens do a lot of business over the Web. You can even use these companies' websites to order prescription refills that you then pick up at your local store.

Lower Prices

Because of the lower costs of doing business online, many online-only drugstores offer lower prices than some brick-and-mortar pharmacies. (Be sure to compare your specific prescription to find the best price.) The trade-off with online pharmacies, of course, is the lack of human interaction. If you need the advice of a pharmacist, use your corner druggist instead.

Shop Online Pharmacies

If you're interested in getting your prescriptions filled online, here are some of the more popular online pharmacies. Most of these sites honor prescriptions from major insurance and HMO plans.

1 The big national pharmacy chains have their own websites for ordering your prescriptions so that you can pick them up at your local store. You can order online from CVS (www.cvs.com), Rite Aid (www.riteaid.com), and Walgreens (www.walgreens.com); you can also access the pharmacy departments of Target (www.target.com/pharmacy/) and Walmart (www.walmart.com/pharmacy/) on the Web.

2 Several "virtual pharmacies" on the Web let you order prescription drugs and have them delivered to your door via the mail. The most popular include Express Scripts (www.express-scripts.com), Familymeds (www.familymeds.com), HealthWarehouse (www.healthwarehouse.com), and RXdirect (www.rxdirect.com). You need to have your doctor fax or email your prescriptions to get started.

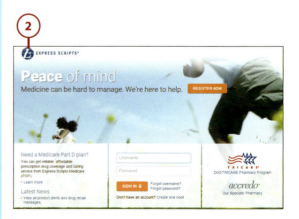

Insurance Plans

Check with your health insurance company to see which online pharmacies are covered under your specific insurance plan.

It's Not All Good

Online Scammers

In addition to the major online pharmacies, there are also hundreds (if not thousands!) of sites selling Viagra, Cialis, and similar drugs online. Most of these sites are based outside the United States and sell generic versions of these and other drugs that are not available in generic form in the U.S. (You see a lot of "Canadian pharmacy" sites online.)

Some of these sites are legitimate. Some aren't. It's easy to get scammed into sending your money to a site that never delivers, or delivers something not quite what you expected. The lower prices of these knock-off drugs are tempting, but in the case of prescription medicine, it's better to be safe than sorry. When in doubt, ask your doctor or insurance provider whether a particular online pharmacy is legit.

In addition, you need to beware of the online equivalent of snake oil salesmen. Numerous websites exist solely to prey on the easily impressionable, offering quack diagnoses and expensive, normally "herbal," remedies. (There are especially large numbers of these sites in the diet arena.) When it comes to sites that offer quick cures for common ailments, stay away. If it sounds too good to be true, it probably is!

In this chapter, you learn how to find fun and engaging games to play over the Internet.

→ Exploring Different Types of Games
→ Finding Online Games

16

Playing Games Online

Games aren't just for kids—especially online games. Whether you like to play a little solitaire, answer trivia questions, or do the latest word quiz, you can find all sorts of fun games to play online. Just launch your web browser and go to one of the many games sites on the Internet, and you'll soon be playing along with the best of them.

Exploring Different Types of Games

You can find just about any type of game online. Some games are single-player; some let you play against other players anywhere in the world—as long as they're connected to the Internet, that is.

Arcade Games

Pac Man (www.webpacman.com)

Many games sites offer online versions of classic and current arcade games that you can play against the computer. Look especially for older arcade games like Asteroids, Battlezone, Centipede, and Pong—as well as newer arcade-like games, like those in the Angry Birds family.

Board Games

Chess (www.chess.com)

No doubt you've played more than a few board games in your life. Many of these online board games let you play either against the computer or with family and friends, in real time online.

Board games online include variations of backgammon, checkers, chess, dominos, and mahjong. You'll also find some commercial board games online, including Monopoly, Scrabble, and Yahtzee.

Family Games

Board games are especially good for playing with your children and grand-children. Most are multiplayer games, so you can take turns or play as a team.

Brain Training Games

Brain-training games may help improve your memory, focus, and comprehension. They're fun to play, too!

You probably won't find a lot of brain-training games at the general games sites that we discuss later in this chapter. Instead, you need to visit dedicated sites, such as Free Brain Age Games (www.freebrainagegames.com), Games for the Brain (www.gamesforthebrain.com), and Senior Brains (www.seniorbrains.com). You can also find a bevy of brain games at the AARP website (www.aarp.org/health/brain-health/brain_games/).

Lumosity

Lumosity (www.lumosity.com) is another popular site that offers a variety of brain games. The site used to claim that its games could help prevent memory loss, dementia, and even Alzheimer's disease. These claims were overreaching, however; there is simply no scientific evidence to prove such results. In fact, the FTC fined Lumosity $2 million for making these false claims. Lumosity still offers fun and interesting games, they just don't have the effect that they once claimed.

Card Games

Solitaire (www.cardgamesolitaire.com)

Card games have always been popular among the 50+ set. (And with youngsters, too!) Tons of card games are available for online play, including variations of bridge, cribbage, euchre, gin rummy, solitaire, and UNO.

Casino Games

Many people, young and old, like to hit the local casinos when they can. Now, with casino games online, you don't have to leave your house to play slots or poker or any other Vegas-style games.

Popular casino games online include variations of bingo, blackjack (21), keno, poker, roulette, and slots. Many online gaming sites offer multiplayer poker and slots tournaments that can actually pay big money. (And cost big money to play, too!)

Poker (www.replaypoker.com)

Puzzle and Matching Games

Bejeweled 3 (www.popcap.com/bejeweled-3)

Puzzle and matching games require you to solve some sort of conundrum or match two or more items to score points. For example, with a match-2 game you have to find two matching items; a match-3 game requires you to find three matching items.

Popular games in this genre include Bejeweled, Candy Crush Saga, Flow Free, and Tetris. Also popular are various jigsaw puzzles and the many variations of Sudoku.

Simulation Games

FarmVille 2 on Facebook

Simulation games let you build your own virtual worlds and then explore and nurture them. They're immersive and can eat up a ton of your time!

The most popular of these games include FarmVille, TrainStation, and Zoo World. Also popular, especially with the younger generations, is Minecraft, which lets users build and explore their own block-like virtual worlds.

Sports Games

If you're a big sports fan, you may also like to play sports games online. Depending on the games site you visit, you're likely to find single- or multiplayer versions of archery, baseball, basketball, bowling, fishing, football, golf, and even pool.

Golf (www.ogcopen.com)

Trivia Games

What was the name of Harry Truman's vice president? What TV show did George Clooney star in before *E.R.*? What is the smallest planet in the solar system? If you know the answers to these questions, you'll have a lot of fun with the many trivia games available online.

You'll find all kinds of trivia games online, including general, entertainment, nostalgia, and sports trivia. There are also online versions of many TV trivia games, too, including Family Feud and Jeopardy!

James Bond trivia (www.triviaplaza.com)

Word Games

Word games, including anagrams and brain teasers, are popular with users of all ages. They're fun to play and require nothing more than a good grasp of language.

The most popular games in this category include Charades, Scrabble, Words with Friends, and many other word-search puzzlers.

Words with Friends on Facebook

>>>*Go Further*

GAMES FOR KIDS

Playing computer games is a good way to keep younger children or grandchildren occupied. When they get bored or whiney, just fire up their favorite games and let them play.

The following websites offer a good selection of online games for kids:

- Angry Birds (www.angrybirds.com/play)
- Disney Games (games.disney.com)
- FunBrain (www.funbrain.com)
- Knowledge Adventure (www.knowledgeadventure.com)
- LEGO Games (www.lego.com/games/)
- Mattel Games (www.mattel.com/games)
- Nick Jr. Games (www.nickjr.com/games/)
- PBS Kids Games (www.pbskids.org/games/)
- PopCap Games (www.popcap.com)
- Sprout Games (www.sproutonline.com/games)

In addition, most of the multigame websites, discussed next, offer a good selection of games for kids.

Finding Online Games

Where do you find games to play online? They're practically everywhere, if you know where to look.

Discover Multigame Websites

Miniclip (www.miniclip.com)

Your best bet for finding a variety of games are the big multigame websites. These sites offer hundreds of games in different categories for your entertainment pleasure.

Playing a game at one of these sites is as simple as clicking the link for the game, clicking the "play" button, and then letting the game load in your web browser. You need to read the instructions first, of course, especially if you need to find an online partner to play a particular game. Don't get too nervous about this, though; most sites make playing these kinds of games extremely simple, and the process practically painless.

Here's a short list of some of the more popular online games sites:

- Addicting Games (www.addictinggames.com)
- Agame (www.agame.com)
- All Games Free (www.allgamesfree.com)
- ArcadeTown (www.arcadetown.com)
- Games.com (www.games.com)
- Gamesgames.com (www.gamesgames.com)
- Gamesville (www.gamesville.com)

- Miniclip (www.miniclip.com)

- Pogo.com (www.pogo.com)

- Yahoo! Games (games.yahoo.com)

AARP Games

The AARP website also offers a large selection of games that are particularly popular with users aged 50 and over. Go to games.aarp.org to start playing!

Find Other Games Online

Candy Crush Saga (www.candycrushsaga.com)

Some of the most popular online games cannot be found at these multigame websites. Instead, the companies behind these games host their own websites; you have to go their sites to play their games.

For example, if you want to play Candy Crush Saga on your computer, you have to go to the Candy Crush Saga website, located at www.candycrushsaga.com. To play Bejeweled Blitz (or any Bejeweled game), go to the PopCap site, at www.popcap.com.

Other popular games are available only for mobile devices, so you can play them on your phone or tablet but not on your computer. Still others can be played on your computer, but only via the Facebook social networking site. So, for example, if you want to play FarmVille or Words with Friends, you either need to install the game on your smartphone or tablet, or sign in to Facebook and play it there.

Bottom line, if you're looking for a specific game online, search for it on Google or Bing. If it's available for online play, you'll see it listed. If not, and you still want to play it, you may need to download it to your mobile phone.

It's Not All Good

In-Game Purchases

Many game sites make money by trying to sell you things within their games. That is, they encourage (or even require) in-game purchases for things like extra in-game currency, more lives, even access to higher levels. In some games, you can't proceed past a certain point without making an in-game purchase. I hate games that require this sort of pay-to-play, especially when my eight-year-old grandson runs into a brick wall that only grandpa's credit card can fix. (Try saying "no" to an eight-year-old; you know what I mean.)

These in-game purchases can also be a little deceiving, especially if you're new to the game. You may think you're just getting more information or moving on naturally and then later find you've been billed for five or ten or more bucks for an in-game purchase. For this reason, be careful what you tap when you're playing an online game—you don't want to spend more money than you expect!

Gmail

Yahoo! Mail

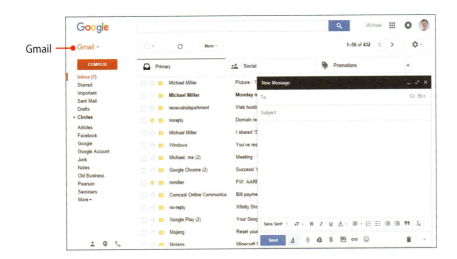

17

Emailing Friends and Family

When it comes to keeping in touch with the people you know and love, the easiest way to do so is via electronic mail, otherwise known as *email*. An email message is like a regular letter, except that it's composed electronically and delivered almost immediately via the Internet. You can use email to send both written messages and file attachments (such as digital photos) to pretty much anyone with an Internet connection.

Understanding How Email Works

Email is like traditional postal mail, except that you compose messages that are delivered electronically via the Internet. When you send an email message to another Internet user, that message travels from your PC to your recipient's PC through a series of Internet connections and servers, almost instantaneously. Email messages can be of any length and can include file attachments of various types.

Email Addresses

To make sure your message goes to the right recipient, you have to use your recipient's *email address.* Every Internet user has a unique email address, composed of three parts:

- The user's name
- The @ sign
- The user's domain name (usually the name of the Internet service provider, or ISP)

As an example, if you use Comcast as your Internet provider (with the domain name comcast.net) and your login name is jimbo, your email address is jimbo@comcast.net.

POP/IMAP Email

There are actually two different ways to send and receive email via the Internet—POP/IMAP email and web-based email.

The traditional way to send and receive email uses a protocol called the Post Office Protocol (POP), which routes email through your ISP to an email app on your computer. It's similar to the newer Instant Message Access Protocol (IMAP) that offers a few more options for synchronizing messages between different devices.

To send or receive POP/IMAP email, you have to use a special email program, such as Microsoft Outlook (part of the Microsoft Office suite) or the Mail app included with Windows 10. That email program has to be configured to send email to your ISP's outgoing mail server (called an *SMTP server*) and to receive email from your ISP's incoming mail server (called a *POP3* or *IMAP server*). If you want to access your email account from another computer, you have to use a similar email program and go through the entire configuration process all over again on the second computer.

POP/IMAP Email in Your Browser

Many POP/IMAP email providers also offer web-based access from any web browser.

Web-Based Email

As you can see, using POP/IMAP email requires a separate app and a lot of configuration. An easier way to get your email is over the Web via web-based email services, such as Google's Gmail and Yahoo! Mail. Unlike straight POP/IMAP email, you can access web-based mail from any computer, using any web browser; no special software is required.

If you use a PC in multiple locations—in the office, at home, or on the road—this is a convenient way to check your email at any time of day, no matter where you are. With web-based mail, you can also check your email from your smartphone or tablet; the device you use doesn't matter.

Another plus is that web-based email doesn't require the same sort of complicated configuration routine that you need with POP/IMAP email. All you have to do is go to the email service's website, enter your user ID and password, and you're ready to send and receive messages.

Most web-based mail services are completely free to use. Some services offer both free versions and paid versions, with paid subscriptions offering additional message storage and functionality.

The largest web mail services include the following:

- AOL Mail (webmail.aol.com)
- Gmail (mail.google.com)
- Mail.com (www.mail.com)
- Outlook.com (www.outlook.com)
- Yahoo! Mail (mail.yahoo.com)

These services let you send and receive email from any computer connected to the Internet via your web browser. (You can also connect via mobile apps on your smartphone or tablet.) They're ideal if you travel a lot or maintain two homes in different locations. (Snowbirds rejoice!!)

Emailing with Gmail

We start by looking at the largest web-based email service, Google's Gmail. You can use any web browser to access your Gmail account and send and receive email from any connected computer, tablet, or smartphone.

Receive and Reply to Messages

To sign up for a new account (it's free), use your web browser to go to mail. google.com. You can then send and receive email from any computer just by signing in to your Google account.

1 Click the Inbox link to display all incoming messages.

2 Gmail organizes your email into types, each with its own tab: Primary, Social (messages from Facebook, Google+, and similar social networks), and Promotions (advertising messages). Most of your messages will be in the Primary tab, so click that or another tab you want to view.

3 Click the header for the message you want to view.

4 To download an attached folder or file, mouse over the item and then click the Download icon.

5 To reply to an open message, click Reply. (To reply to all recipients of a message, click the down arrow next to Reply and select Reply to All.)

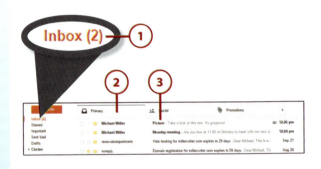

6 Enter your reply text in the message window.

7 Click Send when done.

It's Not All Good

Don't Click Unexpected Attachments

While you *can* click to open an email attachment, that doesn't mean you should. In fact, unless you are expecting that specific attachment from an individual, you should *not* click to open attachments.

I repeat, do *not* click unexpected email attachments.

Here's why.

Unscrupulous users can implant malicious software—what we call *malware*—inside file attachments. When you click to open a malicious attachment, something bad happens in the form of a computer virus or spyware. That is, you click a file attachment and your computer gets infected. From there, who knows what happens. Maybe your computer will quit working. Maybe your important files and programs will get deleted. Maybe your computer will be hijacked and used as a *zombie computer* in a computer attack on some website.

The point is, bad things come in unsuspected email attachments. What might look like a photograph or Word document or ZIP file actually contains malware that will, as the name implies, do malicious things to your computer system. Click a file and bad things *will* happen.

For this reason, you should only open file attachments from people you know and that you are expecting. (Unfortunately, even your friend's computer can be hijacked by malware into sending out more malware to people on his contacts list.) Don't trust any file attachment you weren't expecting.

Period.

Send a New Message

New messages you send are composed in a New Message pane that appears at the bottom right corner of the Gmail window.

1 Click Compose from any Gmail page to display the New Message pane.

2 Enter the email address of the recipient(s) in the To box. To send to multiple recipients, separate the addresses with a comma, like this: **books@internet.com, papers@internet.com**

3 Enter a subject in the Subject box.

4 Move your cursor to the main message area and type your message.

5 Send the message by clicking the Send button.

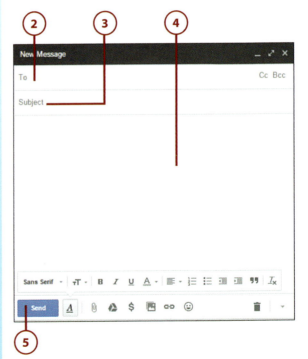

Cc: and Bcc:

Gmail also lets you send carbon copies (Cc:) and blind carbon copies (Bcc:) to additional recipients. (A blind carbon copy is not visible to other recipients.) Just click the **Cc** or **Bcc** links to add these addresses.

Send a File as an Attachment

One of the easiest ways to share a digital photo or other file with another person is via email as an *attachment* to a standard email message. When the message is sent, the file travels along with it; when the message is received, the file is right there, waiting to be opened.

(1) Start with a new message and then click Attach Files.

(2) Navigate to and select the file you want to send.

(3) Click Open.

(4) Complete and send the message as normal by clicking the Send button.

Large Files

Avoid sending extra-large files (2 MB or more) via email. They can take a long time to upload from your computer, and just as long for the recipient to download when received. Even worse, some email systems simply won't send files that are too big. So keep your attachments manageable, if you can.

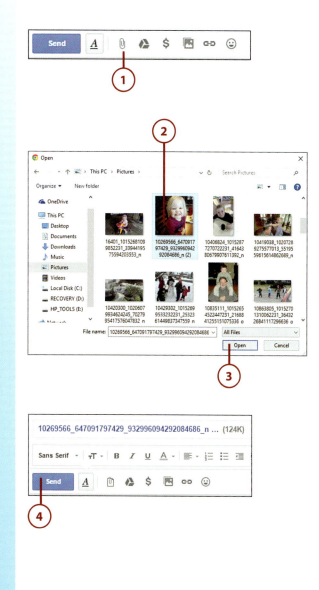

Emailing with Yahoo! Mail

Yahoo! Mail is another popular web-based email service. Many ISPs set up Yahoo! Mail accounts for their customers, so it's possible you may already be using this service.

Receive and Reply to Messages

To create a new Yahoo! Mail account (it's free), point your web browser to mail.yahoo.com. You can then send and receive email from any computer, just by logging in to your account.

1. Click Inbox in the left-hand sidebar to display all incoming messages.

2. Click the header for the message you want to view.

3. To view an attached photograph, click the thumbnail image.

4. To download an attached file, mouse over the item and then click Download.

5. To reply to an open message, click Reply.

6. To reply to all recipients of a group message, click Reply to All.

7. Enter your reply text in the message window.

8. Click Send when done.

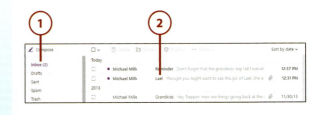

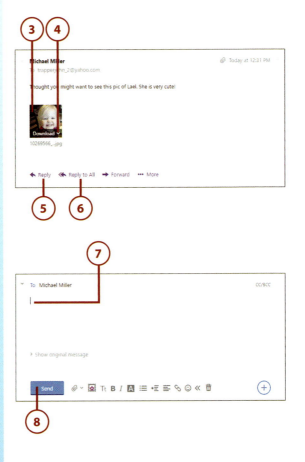

Send a New Message

To send a new message, make sure you have the recipients' email addresses handy.

1 Click Compose in the left-hand sidebar to display a new, blank message.

2 Enter the email address of the recipient(s) in the To box. To send to multiple recipients, separate the addresses with a comma, like this: **books@ internet.com, papers@ internet.com**

3 Enter a subject in the Subject box.

4 Move your cursor to the main message area and type your message.

5 Send the message by clicking the Send button.

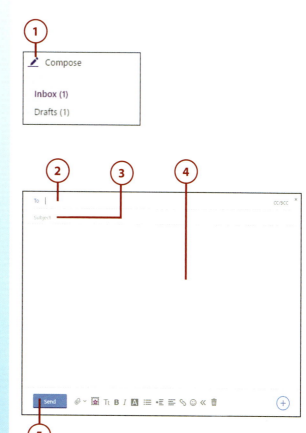

Cc: and Bcc:

Yahoo! Mail also lets you send carbon copies (Cc:) and blind carbon copies (Bcc:) to additional recipients. Just click the **CC/BCC** link to add these addresses.

Send a File as an Attachment

Just like Gmail, Yahoo! Mail also lets you send photos and other files as attachments to your messages.

(1) Start with a new message and then click Attach File beneath the message. This opens the Open window.

(2) Navigate to and select the file you want to attach.

(3) Click Open.

(4) Complete and send the message as normal by clicking the Send button.

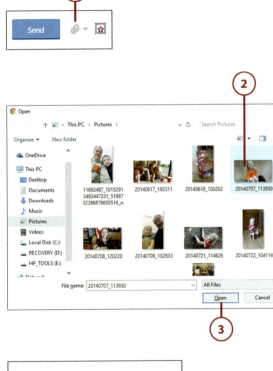

Skype —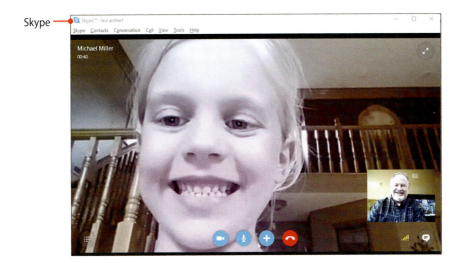

Google
Hangouts —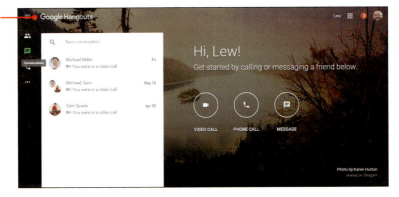

In this chapter, you learn how to make voice and video calls over the Internet with Skype and Google Hangouts.

→ Video Calling with Skype
→ Video Calling with Google Hangouts

18

Video Chatting with Friends and Family

If you travel a lot, live in a different place from family or friends, or winter in warmer climes, you often find yourself far away from the people you love. Just because you're far away, however, doesn't mean that you can't stay in touch—on a face-to-face basis.

When you want to talk to your family members and other loved ones, nothing beats a video call. All you need is a webcam built in to or connected to your computer and a service that lets you make face-to-face calls. Fortunately, there are two such services—Skype and Google Hangouts. Either service is so easy to use that even your grandkids can call you.

Video Calling with Skype

Skype is a service that enables subscribers to connect with one another over the Internet in real time. You can use Skype to conduct one-on-one text chats, audio conversations, and video chats.

To conduct a video call, both you and the person you want to talk to must have webcams built in to or connected to your PCs. In addition, you both must be connected to the Internet for the duration of the call.

To use Skype for video calling, you must first download and install the free Skype application, available from www.skype.com. Once you have the app installed, you can then create your own Skype account. (You can also sign in to Skype with an existing Microsoft account, if you have one.)

The basic Skype service is free and lets you make one-on-one voice and video calls to other Skype users. You can also use Skype to call landline and mobile (non-Skype) phones, for 2.3 cents/minute; monthly subscriptions are also available if you do a lot of non-Skype calling.

Skype and Microsoft

Formerly an independent company, Skype was acquired by eBay in 2005 and then by Microsoft in 2011. Skype currently has more than 300 million users each month.

Add a Contact

Before you call someone with Skype, you have to add that person to your Skype contacts list.

1. From within the Skype app, enter into the search box (in the top-left column) the actual name or Skype username of the person you want to locate and then press Enter or click the Search Skype button.

2 When the search results appear, click the name of the person you want to add.

3 Click the Add to Contacts button.

4 You now have to send a contact request to this person. Enter a short message into the text box, or accept the default message.

5 Click Send. If the person accepts your request, you are added to each other's contact lists.

Accepting Contact Requests

Just as you can request someone to be your contact, other people can send contact requests to you. You have the option of accepting or declining any such request. Make sure it's someone you know before you accept.

Make a Video Call

The whole point of Skype is to let you talk to friends and family. You can use Skype to make voice-only calls or to make video calls—which are great for seeing your loved ones, face to face.

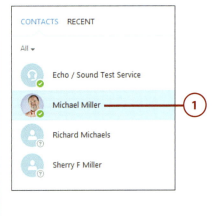

(1) From within the Skype app, go to the Contacts section and click the name of the person you want to call. (People who are online and ready to chat have a solid green dot next to their name.)

(2) Click the Video Call (camera) button at the top-right corner of the window.

(3) Skype now calls this person. When she answers the call, her live picture appears in the main part of the screen. (Your live picture appears smaller, in the lower-right corner.) Start talking!

(4) When you're done talking, click the red "hang up" button to end the call.

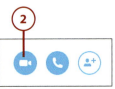

Your picture

>>>Go Further

WEBCAMS

Most notebook computers have webcams built in. You can use your notebook's built-in webcam to make video calls with Skype or Google Hangouts. Because the webcam includes a built-in microphone, you can also use it to make voice calls.

If you have a desktop or all-in-one computer that doesn't have a built-in webcam, you can purchase and connect an external webcam to make video calls. Webcams are manufactured and sold by Logitech and other companies, and connect to your Windows or Mac computer via USB. They're inexpensive (as low as $30 or so) and sit on top of your monitor. After you've connected it, just smile into the webcam and start talking.

Make a Voice Call

If you don't have a webcam attached to your computer, or if you'd rather talk to a person without seeing him, you can use Skype to make a voice call. To do this, you both need micro-phones and speakers attached to your PC, or you can use a USB head-set with a built-in microphone.

(1) From within the Skype app, go to the Contacts section and click the tile for the person you want to call.

(2) Click the Call (telephone) button at the top-right corner of the window. Skype calls this person.

3 When the other person answers the call, you're ready to start talking.

4 Click the red "hang up" button to end the call.

FaceTime

If you use a Mac computer or Apple iPhone or iPad, you can video call with Apple's FaceTime app. FaceTime works much like Skype and Google Hangouts, but only between Apple computers and devices.

Video Calling with Google Hangouts

Not to be outdone by Microsoft (which owns Skype), tech giant Google also offers video chatting. Google Hangouts are real-time video chats you can participate in either one-on-one or with a group of people. All you need is a Google account—and a webcam on your computer, of course.

Start a Video Hangout

To start a hangout, point your web browser to hangouts.google.com and, if you're not already signed in, sign in with your Google account.

1 Click the Conversations icon to view all your previous conversations. To resume a previous video or voice call, click that conversation in the list.

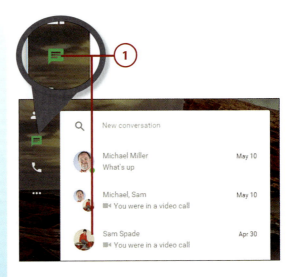

2 To start a new video call, click the Contacts icon to display your list of contacts.

3 Click the name of the person you want to talk with.

4 A new Hangouts window opens on your desktop. Click the Video Call icon.

5 When your friend answers the call, her picture appears large in the Hangouts window. Your picture appears smaller, at the bottom. Start chatting.

6 To exit the hangout, mouse over the window and click the Leave Call button.

Group Hangouts

You can create hangouts with more than two people participating. To add other people to a video call, mouse over the video window and click the Invite People button. When the next dialog box appears, enter the names of the people you want to invite into the Send Invite box and then click the Invite button.

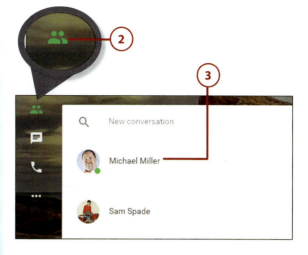

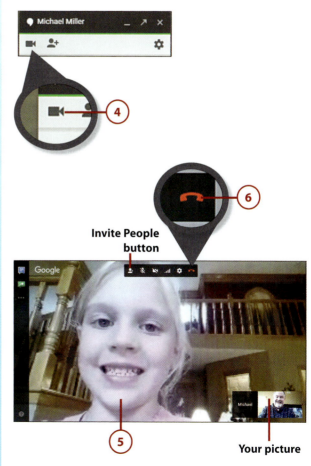

Invite People button

Your picture

Make a Voice Call

Google Hangouts also let you make voice calls to any landline or mobile phone. Most U.S. and Canadian calls are free; international calls cost a little.

1. From the main Google Hangouts page, click the Phone Calls icon.

2. Click a contact from your list to place a call, or…

3. Enter the phone number manually at the top of the contacts pane and then click Call.

4. You now see a dialer pane on the right, and the call is made. To end the call, click the Hang Up button.

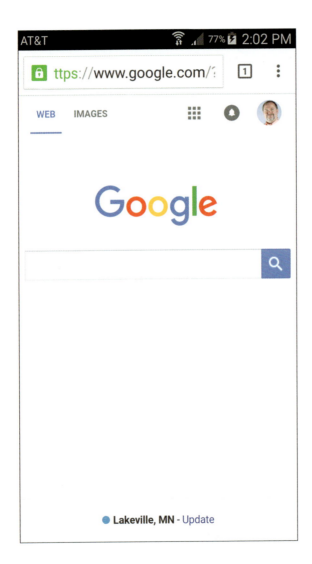

Exploring the Mobile Internet with Your Smartphone or Tablet

Throughout this book we've primarily discussed ways to use the Internet with your desktop or notebook/laptop computer. Well, you can also go online from your smartphone or tablet—and access the Internet from just about anywhere.

Connecting and Browsing on an iPhone or iPad

Apple makes some of the most popular mobile phones and tablets today. All Apple iPhones and iPads easily connect to nearby Wi-Fi networks and hotspots, and thus to the Internet.

It's Not All Good

Internet via Data Connection

Most smartphones also let you connect to the Internet via your mobile data connection (from your cellular provider). This lets you connect when there are no nearby Wi-Fi networks.

The problem with connecting to the Internet via a mobile data connection is that most cellular providers charge extra for their data plans. You typically get a set amount of data you can download (for a set price); if you exceed that amount of data, you pay extra—sometimes, a lot extra.

For that reason, you probably want to limit the bulk of your Internet usage to when your phone is connected to a Wi-Fi network, either yours at home or a public one elsewhere. Definitely avoid data-intensive tasks, such as watching videos and downloading large files, when you're on a limited mobile data connection. Save all that for when you're on Wi-Fi.

Connect to a Wi-Fi Network

You can connect your iOS device to both private Wi-Fi networks, like the one you have in your home, and public Wi-Fi hotspots.

1. Tap Settings to display the Settings screen.

2. Tap Wi-Fi to display the Wi-Fi screen.

3 Make sure Wi-Fi is turned on; if not, tap the control to turn it on.

4 Your device now searches for and displays available Wi-Fi networks. Password-protected networks have a lock icon by their names. Tap the name of the Wi-Fi network you want to join.

5 If you selected an open Wi-Fi network, you are now connected. If you selected a password-protected network, enter the password and tap Join.

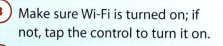

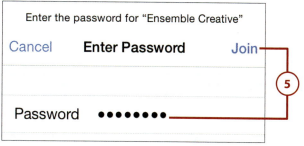

>>>Go Further
SIGNING IN

Private Wi-Fi networks are like the one you have in your home. Private networks typically require you to enter a password to access the network. This password is typically created when you first set up your wireless router, or provided by the network host if you're connecting to an office network.

Public Wi-Fi networks typically do not require a password to connect. However, some public hotspots do require you to manually sign in. In some instances, your phone automatically launches its web browser after you connect to the network, with the host's sign in page displayed. In other cases you have to manually launch your device's web browser and try to open any web page; the host's sign in page is then displayed instead of the normal web page, and you can sign in from there.

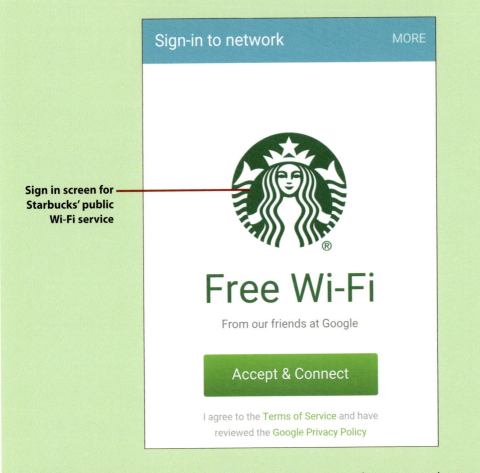

Sign in screen for Starbucks' public Wi-Fi service

Some sign in pages ask you to agree to the host's terms of service as to how you'll use the connection. Others just want you to click the "sign in" button. Whatever the case, do what's asked of you so you can sign in and get started on the Internet.

Browse the Web with Safari

Apple includes its own Safari web browser with all its iOS devices. You use Safari to visit web pages on your iPhone or iPad.

1 Tap the Safari icon to open the Safari browser.

2 Tap within the Address box to display the onscreen keyboard; then enter the address of the web page you want to visit.

3 As you type, Safari suggests matching web pages. Tap any page to go to it *or…*

4 Finish entering the full address and then tap Go on the keyboard to go to that page.

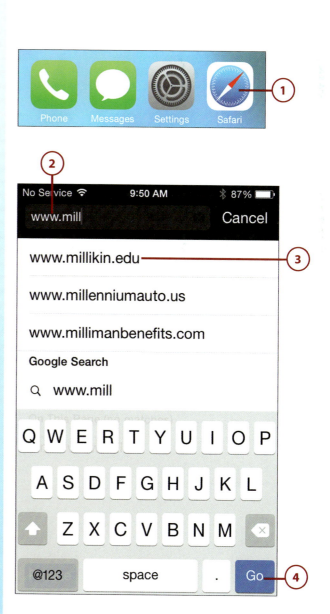

5 The web page appears onscreen. Swipe up to scroll down the page.

6 If a page has trouble loading, of if you want to refresh the content, tap the Reload button.

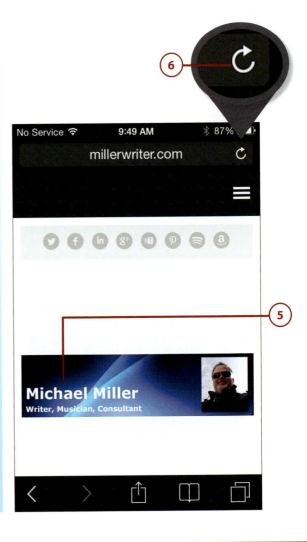

Mobile Websites

Many (but not all) websites today offer mobile versions of their sites, especially configured for the confines of smaller phone and tablet screens. The mobile version of a site should appear automatically when you click to or enter a site's normal URL. If a site does not have a mobile version, see whether there's a mobile app you can use, instead. (We discuss mobile apps later in this chapter.)

Connecting and Browsing on an Android Phone or Tablet

Connecting to the Internet is similar if you have an Android phone or tablet. You first connect to a private or public Wi-Fi network, which then connects you to the Internet.

Connect to a Wi-Fi Network

When your phone is near an active Wi-Fi network or hotspot, you see a "not connected" icon in the status bar. (And if you're on the Lock screen, you see a notification about "Wi-Fi networks available.") You choose which Wi-Fi network to connect to and then you connect to it.

1 Swipe down from the top of the screen to display the notification panel.

2 Tap the Wi-Fi Networks Available notification or…

3 Tap and hold the Wi-Fi icon.

1

11:36 AM Wed, May 6

Wi-Fi   Location   Sound   Screen   Bluetooth
                                rotation

Auto

Wi-Fi networks available   **2**
Tap to view available networks.

Verizon Wireless   ⬅ Clear

3

4 You now see the Wi-Fi screen, with available Wi-Fi networks listed in descending order of signal strength. Open networks (those that don't require a password) have a basic icon, whereas private networks that do require a password have a lock on the icon. Tap the network to which you want to connect.

5 If you're connecting to a public network, you may see a panel for that network warning that information sent over this network may be available to others. This is normal with most public hotspots, and nothing to be concerned about. Tap Connect to connect to the network.

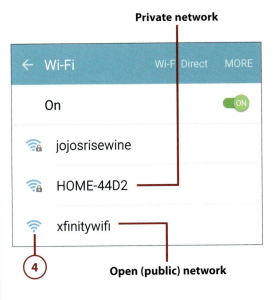

Private network

← Wi-Fi   Wi-Fi Direct   MORE

On   ON

🔒 jojosrisewine

🔒 HOME-44D2

xfinitywifi

4   Open (public) network

xfinitywifi

You are connecting to the unsecure network "xfinitywifi". Information sent is not encrypted and may be visible to others. Do you still want to connect?

☐ Show advanced options

CANCEL   CONNECT —**5**

6 If you're connecting to a private network, you see a panel for that network and the onscreen keyboard appears. Use the onscreen keyboard to enter the network's password into the Password box. (Tap Show Password if you want to see the actual characters as you type; otherwise, you just see dots.)

7 Tap Connect. You're now connected to the network and can start using the Internet.

Ensemble Creative

Password

•••••••

☐ Show password

☐ Show advanced options

CANCEL   CONNECT

Connect to a Wi-Fi Network You've Used Before

When you're in range of a Wi-Fi network that you've connected to before, you don't have to do anything. Because your phone remembers the networks you've connected to, it automatically connects to this familiar network.

Browse the Web with Chrome

Most Android phones and tablets come with Google's Chrome web browser preinstalled. The version of Chrome on your smartphone or tablet is similar to the version you might be using on your personal computer, but it's customized to the smaller phone display.

1. From any Home screen, tap the Chrome icon to open Google Chrome.

2. Tap within the Omnibox to display the onscreen keyboard. If the Omnibox is not visible (it slides up when not in use), drag down the web page until it appears.

3. Enter the address of the web page you want to visit.

4. As you type, Chrome suggests matching web pages. Tap any page to go to it *or...*

5. Finish entering the full address and then tap Go on the keyboard to go to that page.

6 The web page appears onscreen. Swipe up to scroll down the page.

7 If a page has trouble loading, of if you want to refresh the content, you can reload the page. Begin by tapping the Menu button.

8 Tap the Reload button.

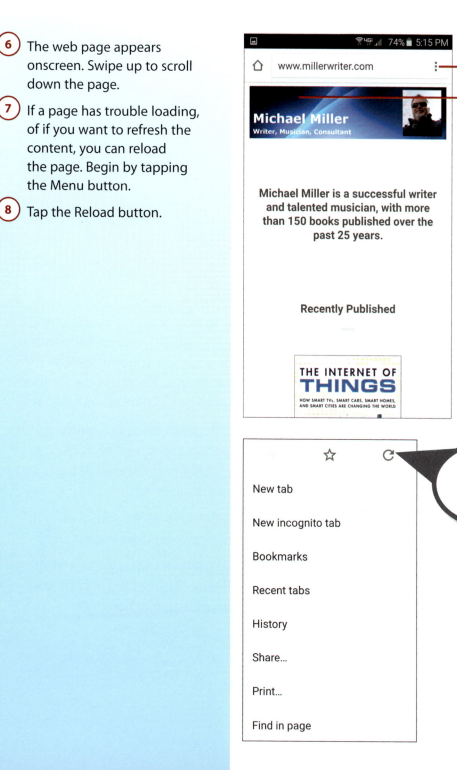

>>>*Go Further*

ZOOM IN TO A PAGE

If you have trouble reading the small type unfortunately found on many websites, you can zoom in to a page. This makes the entire page—including the type you read—bigger.

To zoom in to a page in either the Safari or Chrome browser, press two fingers together on the screen and then spread them apart. In some instances, you can zoom in to a picture or other onscreen item by double tapping it.

To zoom back out, press two fingers apart on the screen and pinch them together.

Discovering Essential Mobile Apps

You can use your mobile device's web browser to do just about everything you can do with your computer's web browser. However, many websites offer dedicated mobile apps that make it easier to access their content and use their services. In these instances, it makes more sense to install and use the mobile app instead of using your mobile browser to go to that organization's website.

For example, while you can use your mobile browser to go to the Netflix website and watch movies and TV shows, the Netflix mobile app is a lot easier to use. Same thing with Pandora and Gmail and many other popular sites. If there's a site you like, there's probably a mobile app you can install instead.

Most companies make their mobile apps available for free. All you have to do is search your device's app store for the apps you want and then install them.

Next, we look at some of the more popular and useful Internet-related mobile apps you may want to install on your mobile device. Most of these apps are available in both iOS (Apple) and Android versions, and most are free.

Email Apps

Google's Gmail app —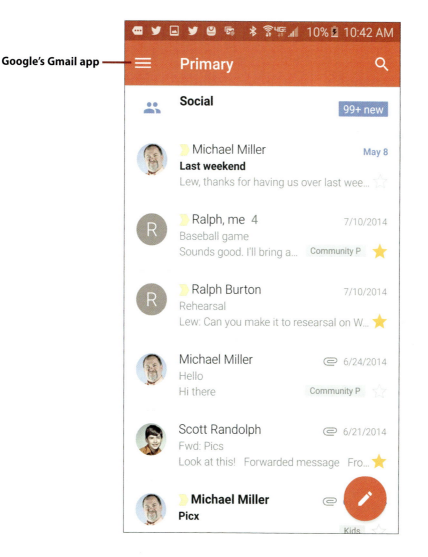

It's likely that your phone or tablet came with its own mail app preinstalled. In most cases, you can configure this app to retrieve POP/IMAP email, as well as connect to most web-based email services.

That said, most web-based email services also offer their own apps, which are more finely tuned to the features and functionality of their own services. The most popular of these apps include the following:

- **Gmail.** The official app for Google's web-based email service.

- **Yahoo! Mail.** The official app for Yahoo!'s web-based email service.

Social Media Apps

Facebook mobile app ———

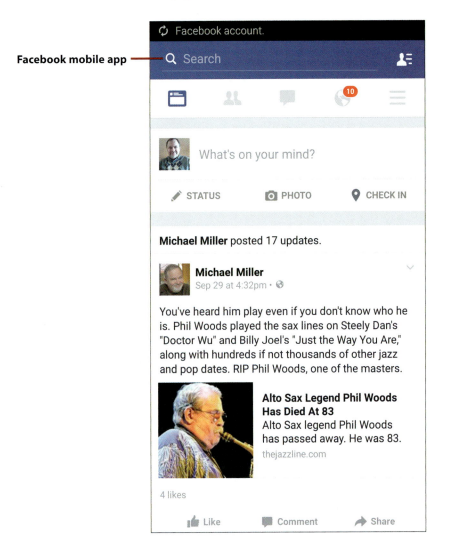

All of today's social networks have their own mobile apps. You want to install the app for each social network you use.

You can find mobile apps available for the following social networks:

- **Facebook.** Perhaps the most-used mobile app today. It does just about everything you can do from Facebook's website, but optimized for smartphone use.

- **Facebook Messenger.** If you send private messages or text chats on Facebook, you need the separate Messenger app. (Private messaging is not built in to the main Facebook mobile app.)

- **Instagram.** The Instagram app lets you share the photos you take over the Instagram social network. The app also functions as a standalone photo app, complete with interesting photo filters and effects.

- **LinkedIn.** Manage your business connections with the official LinkedIn mobile app.

- **Pinterest.** The official Pinterest app lets you review and repin your friends' pins, as well as pin your own pins.

- **Twitter.** This app lets you read your Twitter feed and make your own tweets from the palm of your hand.

Video Chat Apps

It's great to be able to chat with a friend or family member, in real time, on your phone or tablet. We're talking video chats here, so you can see who you're talking to. Check out these mobile apps:

Skype mobile app

- **FaceTime.** FaceTime is an Apple-only app and service, which means you can use it to talk to other iPhone and iPad users, but not to anyone with an Android device. Still, it's well integrated into the Apple system—and installed by default on all Apple devices.

- **Google Hangouts.** Even though this is a Google app and service, it's available for both Android and iOS devices.

- **Skype.** Skype is owned by Microsoft but has mobile apps for both Android and iOS devices.

Streaming Video Apps

Netflix mobile app ———

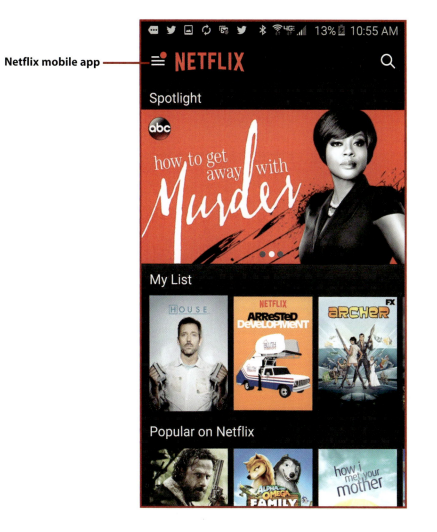

You'd be surprised how many people watch videos on their phones and tablets. Instead of using your web browser to visit streaming video sites, you can use the sites' mobile apps to make viewing that much easier.

Check out the mobile apps for

- **Hulu.** Watch your favorite TV shows on the official Hulu app. (Paid membership required.)

- **Netflix.** The official mobile app for the largest streaming video service today lets you watch your favorite movies and TV shows on your smartphone or tablet. (Paid membership required.)

- **YouTube.** Watch all your favorite videos and upload your own with this video sharing app.

Streaming Music Apps

Pandora mobile app ——

Listening to streaming music on your smartphone is this generation's equivalent of listening to the top forty on your transistor radio back in the day. When you want to listen to music today, just make sure your phone is connected to the Internet, plug in your earphones, and fire up your favorite streaming music app.

Here are the most popular apps for music lovers:

- **Pandora.** The official app for Pandora's free music service; create your own radio stations and listen away.

- **Spotify.** You can use the Spotify app for free, but you get a lot more functionality (including the ability to dial up specific songs) with a paid subscription.

- **TuneIn Radio.** Use the TuneIn app to listen to AM and FM radio stations from around the globe.

Shopping Apps

Most major retailers offer their own (free) apps to make shopping easier on your mobile device. In most cases, the app optimizes the shopping experience for the smaller smartphone screen.

And it's not just online retailers. Many brick-and-mortar stores, such as CVS and Starbucks, have mobile apps that let you pay or use their frequent shopper program from your mobile phone. Just launch the app, navigate to the payment screen, and use the onscreen barcode to pay at the counter.

CVS mobile app —

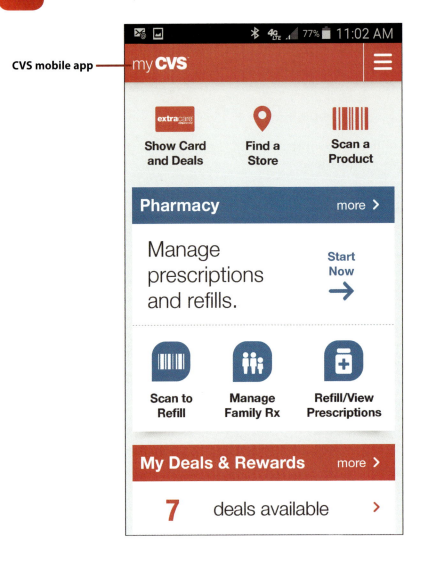

Check out the apps for these retailers:

- Amazon
- Caribou Coffee
- CVS
- Starbucks
- Target
- Walgreens
- Walmart

Other Useful Apps

Tons of other mobile apps let you connect to sites and services on the Web from the comfort of your smartphone or tablet. Check out these apps in your mobile device's app store:

AARP mobile app ——

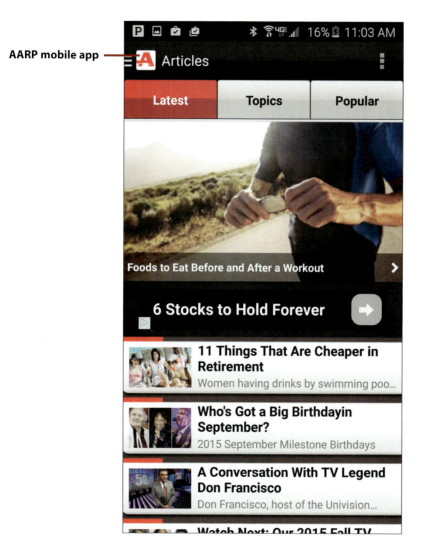

- **AARP.** Use the AARP mobile app to read AARP content on the go, watch video clips, and take advantage of AARP discounts at participating retailers.

- **Ancestry.** Update your family tree while you're on the go with the Ancestry app. (Paid membership required.)

- **CNN.** Get the latest news headlines and stories from the official CNN mobile app.

- **Google Docs, Sheets, and Slides.** Use Google's productivity apps to do word processing, spreadsheets, or presentations from your mobile device. (Three separate apps.)

- **Google Drive.** Use Google Drive to store and access your files in the cloud. Upload files from your PC and access them from your phone or tablet.

- **Google Maps.** One of the most popular mobile apps out there, available for both iOS and Android devices, which lets you generate maps and real-time driving directions on your phone.

- **Microsoft Office Mobile.** Yes, you can work on your Word, Excel, and PowerPoint files from your iOS or Android phone or tablet.

- **The Weather Channel.** Use the official Weather Channel app to view current weather conditions, radar maps, and forecasts.

- **Wikipedia.** Want to look up a pertinent fact? Then use the Wikipedia app to get smarter wherever you happen to be.

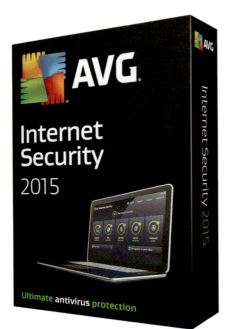

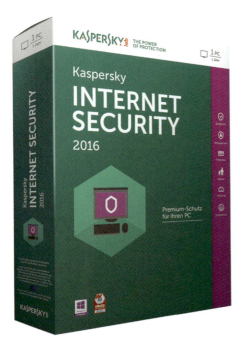

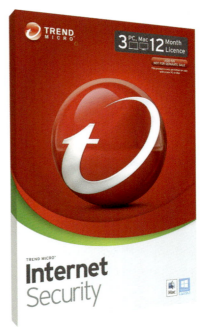

Staying Safe Online

The Internet can be fun. The Internet can be useful. The Internet can be informative.

But the Internet can also be dangerous. It's a place where criminals try to scam unsuspecting people out of their life savings. It's a place where unscrupulous companies attempt to use your personal information for their financial gain. It's a place where malicious hackers try to damage or hijack your computer system.

All that sounds frightening, and it can be, especially for older users. Many online predators specifically target older people, and for good reasons. Many older computer users are more naïve and trusting than younger users, and many are also less tech savvy. In addition, older users often have large nest eggs that are attractive to online predators, and many older people are ashamed to report being taken advantage of.

No matter how smart you are, you can still get scammed online—which means you need to protect yourself. You need to be able to identify the most common online threats and scams, and avoid becoming a victim.

Protecting Against Identity Theft and Phishing Scams

Want to know what most online predators want? It's information—your *personal* information, such as your full name, street address, online usernames and passwords, bank account numbers, ATM PINs, and the like. When a predator gains access to this information, he can use it to hack into your online and offline accounts.

What happens next is called *identity theft*. This phrase is a catch-all for any crime, no matter how minor, involving the illegal use of your individual identity in any form.

Identity theft can be the result of online negligence (responding to phishing emails or being the victim of a computer virus) or real-world theft (having your wallet stolen or credit card statements pilfered from your trash). However it happens, the identity thief obtains your valuable personal information and then uses that information to access your social media and other accounts and pose as you online, make unauthorized charges on your credit card, and maybe even drain your bank account.

There are many ways for criminals to obtain your personal information. Almost all involve tricking you, in some way or another, into providing this information of your own free will. Your challenge is to avoid being tricked.

Identity Theft Is Real

Make no mistake about it, identity theft is a major issue. According to Javelin Strategy and Research, more than 12 million American adults were victims of identity theft in 2015, with a new victim every two seconds. A typical case of identity theft costs the average victim more than $5,000.

Avoid Phishing Scams

Online, identity thieves often use a technique called *phishing* to trick you into disclosing valuable personal information. It's called that because the other party is "fishing" for your personal information, typically via fake email messages and websites.

A phishing scam typically starts with a phony email message that appears to be from a legitimate source, such as your bank, the postal service, PayPal, or other official institution. This email purports to contain important information that you can see if you click the enclosed link. That's where the bad stuff starts.

If you click the link in the phishing email, you're taken to a fake website masquerading as the real site, complete with logos and official-looking text. You're encouraged to enter your personal information into the forms on this fake web page; when you do so, your information is sent to the scammer, and you're now a victim of identity theft.

How can you avoid falling victim to a phishing scam? There are several things you can do:

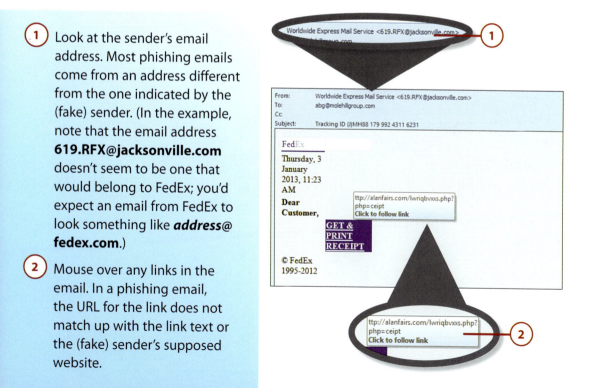

1. Look at the sender's email address. Most phishing emails come from an address different from the one indicated by the (fake) sender. (In the example, note that the email address **619.RFX@jacksonville.com** doesn't seem to be one that would belong to FedEx; you'd expect an email from FedEx to look something like **address@ fedex.com**.)

2. Mouse over any links in the email. In a phishing email, the URL for the link does not match up with the link text or the (fake) sender's supposed website.

3 Look for poor grammar and misspellings. Many phishing schemes come from outside the U.S. by scammers who don't speak English as their first language. As such, you're likely to find questionable phrasing and unprofessional text—not what you'd expect from your bank or other professional institution.

4 If you receive an unexpected email, no matter the apparent source, do **not** click any of the links in the email. If you think there's a legitimate issue from a given website, go to that site manually in your web browser and access your account from there.

5 Some phishing messages include attached files that you are urged to click to display a document or image. Do **not** click or open any of these attachments; they might contain malware that can steal personal information or damage your computer. (Read more about malware later in this chapter.)

Anti-Phishing Filters

Many web browsers—including Google Chrome, Internet Explorer, and Microsoft Edge—offer some built-in protection against phishing scams in the form of filters that alert you to potential phishing sites. If you click a bad link or attempt to visit a known or suspected phishing site, the browser displays a warning message. Do not enter information into these suspected phishing sites—return to your home page, instead!

Keep Your Private Information Private

Identity theft can happen any time you make private information public. This has become a special issue on social networks, such as Facebook, where some users seem to forget that everything they post is publicly visible.

Many Facebook users not only post personal information in their status updates but also include sensitive data in their personal profiles. Javelin Strategy and Research found that 68% of people with public social media profiles shared their birthday information, 63% shared the name of their high school, 18% shared their phone number, and 12% shared their pet's name.

None of this might sound dangerous, until you realize that all these items are the type of personal information many companies use for the "secret questions" their websites use to reset users' passwords. A fraudster armed with this publicly visible information could log on to your account on a banking website, for example, reset your password (to a new one he provides), and thus gain access to your banking accounts.

The solution to this problem, of course, is to enter as little personal information as possible when you're online. For example, you don't need to—and shouldn't—include your street address or phone number in a comment or reply to an online news article. Don't give the bad guys anything they can use against you!

1 Unless absolutely necessary, do not enter your personal contact information (home address, phone number, and so on) into your social media profile.

2 Do not post or enter your birthdate, children's names, pets' names, and the like—anything that could be used to reset your passwords at various websites.

3 Do not post status updates that indicate your current location—especially if you're away from home. That's grist for both physical stalkers and home burglars.

Hide Personal Information on Facebook

Facebook is the world's largest social network, and the social network most used by those 50 and over, so it bears some special attention. That's especially so when you realize that too many Facebook users of all ages make all their personal information totally public—visible to all users, friends or not. Fortunately, you can configure Facebook's privacy settings to keep your private information private.

1. Click your name in the Facebook toolbar to open your personal Timeline page.

2. Click the Update Info button.

3. Mouse over the information you want to make public and then click Edit.

4. Click the Privacy button for the individual item you want to change.

5. Select Friends to make this information visible only to people on your friends list—or click Only Me to completely hide this information from others. Click Save Changes when done.

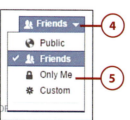

Make Your Facebook Posts Private

You can configure Facebook to hide your status updates from anyone not on your friends list. You can also configure the privacy settings for each individual post you make on Facebook. This way you can post more personal information only to select friends and hide it from the general public.

1. Click the Privacy Shortcuts button on the Facebook Toolbar to display the pull-down menu.

2. Select Who Can See My Stuff? to expand the pull-down menu.

3. Pull down the Who Can See My Future Posts? list and select Friends.

4. To change who can see any individual status update, create a new post, click the Privacy button, and make a new selection: Public, Friends, or Only Me. This setting will be applied to this and all future posts until or unless you change it again.

Custom Privacy

To hide posts from select individuals, select Custom in the Privacy list and then enter the names of people you don't want to share with. Finish by clicking Save Changes.

Protecting Against Online Fraud

Identity theft isn't the only kind of online fraud you might encounter. Con artists are especially creative in concocting schemes that can defraud unsuspecting victims of thousands of dollars.

Most of these scams start with an email message that promises something for nothing. Maybe the message tells you that you've won a lottery, or you are asked to help someone in a foreign country deposit funds in a U.S. bank account. You might even receive requests from people purporting to be far-off relatives who need some cash to bail them out of some sort of trouble.

The common factor in these scams is that you're eventually asked to either send money (typically via wire transfer) or provide your bank account information—with which the scammers can drain your money faster than you can imagine. If you're naïve or gullible enough, the damage can be considerable.

Protecting yourself from the huge number of these online scams is both difficult and simple. The difficulty comes from the sheer number of scams and their amazing variety. The simplicity comes from the fact that the best way to deal with any such scam is to use common sense—and ignore it.

Scams Are Not Spam

You can't rely on your email program's spam filter to stop scam emails. Spam and scams are two different things, even if they're both unwanted. Although some scam messages will be stopped by spam filters, many messages will get through the filter and land in your inbox, just as if they were legitimate messages—which, of course, they aren't.

Identify Online Scams

Most online fraud is easily detectible by the simple fact that it arrives in your email inbox out of the blue and seems too good to be true. So if you get an unsolicited offer that promises great riches, you know to hit the Delete key—pronto.

Savvy Internet users train themselves to recognize scam emails at a glance. That's because most scam messages have one or more of the following characteristics in common:

(1) The email does not address you personally by name; your name doesn't appear anywhere in the body of the message.

(2) You don't know the person who sent you the message; the message was totally unsolicited.

(3) The message is rife with spelling and grammatical errors. (Scammers frequently operate from foreign countries and do not speak English as their first language.) Conversely, the text of the message might seem overly formal, as if written by someone not familiar with everyday English.

(4) You are promised large sums of money for little or no effort on your part.

(5) You are asked to provide your bank account number, credit card number, or other personal information—or are asked to provide money up front for various fees, or to pay the cost of expediting the process.

{ Strictly Confidental }

(1) Hi

(2) I am Clifford Saravanan , director in charge of Diplomatic sub-contract approvals and payment at Malaysian Ministry of finance.i got your e mail address in the course of my diligent search of internet links containing reputable foreign e mail address.

I have an offer that might interest you which will culminate your financial status perpetua... this offer arose from the Government of Malaysia reserve vault under our care, from which we pay both Indigenous and foreign exe... contract and Sub contra...Payments. I need your assistance to stand as a beneficiary to the sum of us$20,000,000.00 (Twenty, million United States dollars. (3)

(4) I am offering you this Deal because I trust you must be a s...ous and faith... partner, The only th...g needed for this US$ 20 million to be swiftly wired into your account Via payment by Telegraphic under 72 Banking hou... is how swift and...mmitted you will...e in standing as the bonafide sub contractor to this amount of $20 million and a bank account that will be used in accommoda...g this fund, which...e shall legally ac...edited / normalize at the Federal High Court of Justice here in Malaysia.

All modalities are in place to register this transaction as a diplo...tic Sub contract paym...t, w...ch shields it from unnecessary stop orders from several international fund transfer regulatory and monitoring agencies, that usually p...e holds on huge fund...fer in order to request a certain percentage of the fund as fund transfer certification clearance.

Please note that if you desire to accomplish this transaction with me, I advise you to send the followings:Via my private email: cliffordaravanan@e-mail.ua

A: Your Full name B: Your House Address C: Your direct telephone number D: Age E: Occupation. (5)
F: Gender

Waiting for your reply soon. Have a nice day!

Yours Faithfully
Mr.Clifford Saravanan.

Avoid Online Fraud

Recognizing a scam email is just one way to reduce your risk of getting conned online. Here are some more tips you can employ:

- Familiarize yourself with the common types of online scams—and if a message in your inbox resembles any of these common scams, delete it.

- Ignore all unsolicited emails, of any type. No stranger will send you a legitimate offer via email; it just doesn't happen. When you receive an unsolicited offer via email, delete it.

- Don't give in to greed. If an offer sounds too good to be true, it is; there are no true "get rich quick" schemes.

- Never provide any personal information—including credit card numbers, your Social Security number, and the like—via email. If such information is legitimately needed, you can call the company yourself or visit the company's official website to provide the information directly.

More from AARP

For the latest breaking scam alerts and prevention tips, join AARP's Fraud Network (AARP.org/FraudWatchNetwork).

Avoid *Offline* Fraud

Not all computer-based scams are technological in nature. Some use the computer as a MacGuffin of sorts; it's just there to initiate the contact that leads to the eventual fraud.

Let me provide a real-life example of a common computer-based offline fraud. The telephone rings, and the person on the other end identifies himself (typically in broken English) as being from "Windows Support" or even just "Windows." The person says that he's been monitoring your computer and that it's been infected with a computer virus. He then walks you through opening up one or more Windows utilities and directs your attention to all sorts of cryptic messages and error reports. (All of which are real, by the way; a lot of weird stuff goes on behind the scenes of your operating system, much of which looks a little scary if you're not technically inclined.)

Once you're convinced you have a problem, the real scam starts. The caller pressures you into purchasing an anti-virus program to remove the infection, or maybe wants to bill you for removal that he can do over the Internet. The price of this software or service is not cheap; it may run $500 to $1,000. But you really need to buy it, of course, because your computer could quit working at any time. Or so the caller says.

If you're lucky, all you're out is the $500 to $1,000. If you're not lucky, the caller gets you to install real malware on your system (in the guise of the supposed anti-virus program) that sucks more personal information off your hard disk. Or maybe the caller uses the banking information you provide to remove much more than $500 from your checking account.

That's what happened to my mother-in-law. She recently received a call from a person claiming to be from America Online. (She has an AOL email account.) After showing her all the cryptic system messages, they conned her into paying them for services using electronic transfer from her checking account. Well, that's all they needed to drain more than $12,000 from her account. That's not small potatoes.

In her case, there was nothing technical about the scam. No malware was installed on her PC, and no harm was done to her system. (In any case, she doesn't do her banking or other financial transactions online, so there was no data to steal if they wanted to.) The con was of the old-fashioned kind, a smooth-talking operator talking her out of her banking information.

This particular story has a happy ending. My mother-in-law's bank protected her from the scam and eventually redeposited the $12,000 back into her account. (It took a few weeks, however, which made life difficult for her for a time, as you can imagine.) And the bad guys got caught; they were dumb enough to deposit the funds they drained into another account at the same bank.

If you ever receive a call like this, just hang up. Microsoft or America Online or your ISP will never phone you out of the blue and tell you your computer is infected. It just won't happen. Any call of this nature is a con, and you need to ignore it.

If you do happen to take such a call and get scammed like this, contact your bank immediately. They'll know what to do from that point, including contacting the appropriate authorities.

The best protection, however, is simply to use common sense. Don't fall for this kind of scam, either in person, over the telephone, or online. The bad guys depend on victims being naïve enough to go along with their con. You need to be smarter than that.

>>>Go Further

WHAT TO DO IF YOU'VE BEEN SCAMMED

What should you do if you think you've been the victim of an online (or offline) fraud? There are a few steps you can take to minimize the damage:

- If the fraud involved transmittal of your credit card information, contact your credit card company to put a halt to all unauthorized payments—and to limit your liability to the first $50.

- If you think your bank accounts have been compromised, contact your bank to put a freeze on your checking and savings accounts—and to open new accounts, if necessary.

- Contact one of the three major credit reporting bureaus to see whether stolen personal information has been used to open new credit accounts—or max out your existing accounts.

- Contact your local law enforcement authorities—fraud is illegal, and it should be reported as a crime.

- Report the fraud to your state attorney general's office.

- Contact any or all of the following consumer-oriented websites: Better Business Bureau (www.bbb.org), the FBI's Internet Crime Complaint Center (www.ic3.gov), the National Consumers League's Fraud.org site (www.fraud.org), or the Federal Trade Commission's Complaint Assistant (www.ftccomplaintassistant.gov).

Above all, don't provide any additional information or money to the scammers. As soon as you suspect you've been had, halt all contact and cut off all access to your bank and credit card accounts. Sometimes the best you can hope for is to minimize your losses.

Protecting Against Computer Viruses and Other Malware

Any malicious software installed on your computer is dubbed *malware*. There are two primary types of malware—*computer viruses* and *spyware.*

A computer virus is a malicious software program designed to do damage to your computer system by deleting files or even taking over your PC to launch attacks on other systems. A virus attacks your computer when you launch an infected software program, launching a "payload" that often is catastrophic.

Even more pernicious than computer viruses is the proliferation of *spyware*. A spyware program installs itself on your computer and then surreptitiously sends information about the way you use your PC to some interested third party. Spyware typically gets installed in the background when you're installing another program and is almost as bad as being infected with a computer virus. Some spyware programs even hijack your computer and launch pop-up windows and advertisements when you visit certain web pages. If there's spyware on your computer, you definitely want to get rid of it.

Adware: A Special Kind of Spyware

Some spyware, called *adware*, isn't criminal at all; instead it's employed by advertisers and marketers to learn more about your Internet usage. Like other types of spyware, adware is typically placed on your PC when you install some other legitimate software, piggybacking on the main installation. Once installed, the adware works like spyware, monitoring your various activities and reporting back to the host advertiser or marketing firm. The host firm can then use the collected data in a marketing-related fashion—totally unbeknownst to you, of course. Despite its source, adware is still an unwanted intrusion.

Identify a Malware Infection

Most malware infections are recognizable by how they affect the performance of your computer system. Put simply, malware tends to slow down operations on most computers—and sometimes worse. Some malware can cause your web browser to freeze or not work properly; others may actually cause your entire computer to crash. So if your computer is acting slowly or suspiciously, the usual suspect is some sort of malware infection.

In particular, take notice if your computer exhibits any or all of the following behaviors—all symptomatic of a malware infection:

- Your computer runs slowly or exhibits other unusual problems, including system freezes and crashes.

- Your computer has a mind of its own—it sends emails to people in your address book without your knowledge or permission, or shows a lot of hard disk activity (blinking lights) or Internet access when you're not actively using it.

- Your computer's hard disk and/or network activities lights constantly blink or stay lit.

- You get a lot of returned or bounced back emails, caused by the malware program taking control of your email program and using it to mail out loads of spam—without your knowledge or permission.

- You find that your web browser's home page has been changed to another site, without your approval, or you see a strange new toolbar in your web browser.

- When you perform a web search, you end up at some strange site; many malware developers like to send you to a site of their choosing whenever you perform a search.

- You get unexpected pop-up windows onscreen.

- You see one or more strange new sites in the favorites or bookmarks section of your web browser.

If your computer exhibits one or more of these symptoms, you need to run an anti-malware program, discussed next.

Protect Against Malware Infection

You can do several things to avoid having your PC infected with malware. It's all about smart and safe computing.

1. Don't open email attachments from people you don't know— or even from people you do know, if you aren't expecting them. That's because some malware can hijack the address book on an infected PC, thus sending out infected email that the owner isn't even aware of. Just looking at an email message won't harm anything; the damage comes when you open a file attached to the email.

2. Download files only from reliable file archive websites, such as Download.com (download.cnet.com) and Softpedia (www.softpedia.com). Do not download files you find on sites you don't know.

3. Don't access or download files from music and video file-sharing and BitTorrent networks, which are notoriously virus- and spyware-ridden. Instead, download music and movies from legitimate sites, such as the iTunes Store and Amazon MP3 Store.

BitTorrent
BitTorrent is a technology that enables the sharing of large files between individual computers on the Internet. Today, BitTorrent is typically used to illegally share pirated music and movie files.

4 Because viruses and spyware can also be transmitted via physical storage media, share USB drives, CDs, DVDs, and files only with users you know and trust.

Use Anti-Malware Software

No matter how careful you are, if you're online at all your computer can still be at risk for malware infection. For this reason, you need to use anti-malware software to block and remove viruses and spyware from your system.

Here's the good news. If you're using a PC running a recent version of Windows, you already have an anti-malware utility installed. Windows comes with its only anti-malware program, called Windows Defender, and it works pretty well.

That said, you're not locked into using Windows Defender. Other anti-malware solutions are available that work just as well (for both Windows and Mac computers), if not better. These include the following:

- AVG Internet Security (www.avg.com)
- Avira Antivirus (www.avira.com)
- Kaspersky Internet Security (www.kaspersky.com)
- McAfee Internet Security (www.mcafee.com)
- Norton Security (us.norton.com)
- Trend Micro Internet Security (www.trendmicro.com)

If you just purchased a new computer, it might come with a trial version of one of these third-party anti-virus programs preinstalled. That's fine, but know that you'll be nagged to pay for the full version after the 90-day trial. You can do this if you want, but don't need to; remember, you have Windows Defender built in to Windows, and it's both free and effective.

Whichever anti-malware solution you employ, make sure you update it regularly. These updates include information on the latest viruses and spyware, and are invaluable for protecting your system from new threats. Fortunately, most anti-malware programs are configured to update themselves automatically; you may not have to do any manual configuration at all.

Protecting Against Online Attacks and Intrusions

Connecting to the Internet is a two-way street—not only can your computer access other computers online, but other computers can also access your computer. So, unless you take proper precautions, malicious hackers can read your private data, damage your system hardware and software, and even use your system (via remote control) to cause damage to other computers.

Zombie Computers

When a computer is controlled by remote control to attack other computers or send out reams of spam, that computer is said to be a *zombie*. A collection of zombie computers is called a *botnet*.

Employ a Firewall

You protect your system against outside attack by blocking the path of attack with a *firewall*. A firewall is a software program that forms a virtual barrier between your computer and the Internet. The firewall selectively filters the data passed between both ends of the connection and protects your system against outside attack.

If you're running a Mac or Windows PC, there's a firewall built in to the operating system. This firewall is activated by default and is, for most users, more than enough protection against computer attacks.

If you want more protection, employ a third-party firewall program. Most of these programs are more robust and offer more protection than your computer's built-in firewall. The best of these programs include McAfee Total Protection (www.mcafee.com), Norton Security (us.norton.com), and ZoneAlarm Free Firewall (www.zonelabs.com).

Glossary

adware   Spyware used by advertisers and marketers.

anti-malware utility   A piece of software designed to identify, block, and remove computer virus and spyware programs.

Bing   Microsoft's Internet search engine.

bit   The basic unit of information or measurement in computing and digital communications. A bit is digital, which means it's either 1 (on) or 0 (off).

blind carbon copy (bcc:)   When you blind carbon copy an email recipient, he receives a copy of the message, but his name is hidden from other recipients.

bookmark   A means of identifying a web page for future viewing or sharing with other users.

bps   Bits per second, a measurement of Internet connection speeds.

broadband   A faster Internet connection, typically made via cable, DSL, or fiber optic technology.

byte   Eight bits. A byte is typically the smallest addressable unit of measurement in computer memory.

cable Internet   A broadband technology that enables fast Internet connections.

carbon copy (cc:)   When you carbon copy an email recipient, he receives a copy of the email message, and others see his name in the recipient list.

Chrome   Google's web browser.

cloud computing   In cloud computing, computer files and programs are not hosted on individual computers, but rather on a "cloud" of computers accessed via the Internet.

cloud storage   A service, such as Google Drive or Microsoft OneDrive, that stores files on the Internet, accessible from any connected device with a web browser.

comparison shopping site   A site that compares prices from thousands of different online merchants.

computer attack   Any operation executed over the Internet with the intent to disrupt, deny, degrade, or destroy information on a computer or computer network.

computer virus   A software program designed to do damage to your computer system.

cookie   A small text file created by a website and stored on your computer; it records information about your site visit.

denial-of-service attack   Occurs when multiple computers overload a particular computer or web server with thousands of messages at the same time, preventing legitimate users from accessing that website.

dial-up   An Internet connection made via traditional phone lines and limited to 56.6 Kbps.

digital subscriber line (DSL)   Technology that uses standard phone lines to create a broadband Internet connection.

domain name   Together, the second- and top-level domains that identify a specific website. For example, in the URL www.quepublishing.com, **quepublishing.com** is the domain name.

domain name system (DNS)   On the Internet, where all domain names are registered.

downloading   This copies a file from a site on the Internet to your computer. (In contrast, *uploading* a file copies that file from your computer to a site on the Internet.)

Edge   The web browser included in Microsoft Windows 10.

email   Short for "electronic mail," this is a means of sending and receiving letter-like messages via the Internet.

email address   This is necessary to send an email to a recipient; all email addresses are composed of the user's login name, the @ sign, and the user's domain name, like this: **mike@email.com**.

Facebook   The largest social networking site on the Web, Facebook was launched in 2004 and currently has more than 1.5 billion users.

favorite   A way of bookmarking a website you want to visit again in the future.

fiber optic Internet   A broadband connection to the Internet made using pulses of light via fiber optic cable.

file attachment   A file that piggybacks on an email message.

file-sharing networks   These sites let you download music and video files uploaded by other users; they often have illegal copies of music and movies available.

FiOS   Shorthand for Fiber Optic Service. See *fiber optic Internet*.

Firefox   A web browser from Mozilla.

firewall   A piece of software or hardware that acts as a barrier between an individual computer or network and the Internet to prevent unwanted outside access.

flame war   A heated or hostile interaction between two or more people in an online forum.

friend   On a social network, another user with whom you communicate. Most social networks enable you to create lists of friends, who are authorized to view your posts, photographs, and other information.

Gbps   One gigabit (one billion bits) per second.

Google   The Internet's most popular search engine. (And the company behind that search engine—and many other products and services.)

Google Hangouts   Google's web-based video chatting service.

hashtag   A means of indicating an important word in a tweet, similar to identifying a keyword. Hashtags start with a hash character (#) followed by a word or phrase with no spaces. Hashtags are most common on Twitter but are also used on other social media, such as Instagram and Pinterest.

hotspot   A public location that offers wireless Internet access.

hyperlink   A piece of text or a graphic on a web page that, when clicked, links to another page on the Web.

Hypertext Markup Language (HTML)   The coding language used to create all web pages.

identity theft   A form of fraud in which one person pretends to be someone else, typically by stealing personal information, such as a bank account number, credit card number, or Social Security number. The intent of identity theft is often to steal money or obtain other benefits.

IMAP   The Internet Message Access Protocol.

Internet   The global system of interconnected computer systems, a network of networks that links billions of computers and connected devices worldwide.

Internet Explorer   Microsoft's older web browser.

Internet gateway   A device that combines the functionality of an Internet modem and wireless router.

Internet Protocol (IP) address   Used to identify each server and device connected to the Internet.

Internet service provider (ISP)   A company that connects individual users to the Internet backbone—for a fee.

Kbps   One kilobit (1,000 bits) per second.

keyword   A word in a search query that describes something you're looking for.

LinkedIn   A social network for business professionals.

malware   Short for *malicious software*, any computer program designed to infiltrate or damage an infected computer. Computer viruses and spyware are the two most common types of malware.

Mbps   One megabit (one million bits) per second.

microblogging service   A web-based service, such as Twitter or Tumblr, that enables users to post short messages to interested followers in a blog-like format.

mobile app   An application for a smartphone or tablet that performs a specific function.

modem   A piece of equipment used to connect a computer to the Internet by modulating and demodulating an analog signal to and from digital format.

MP3   The most popular compressed audio format, compatible with just about every music player program and portable music player device.

network   A computer network consists of two or more computers or similar devices connected together, typically with the purpose of exchanging information. A local area network connects computers in a single physical location; a wide area network connects computers in multiple locations. The Internet is a very large wide area network.

news feed   On a social network, a collection of posts or status updates from a person's friends.

notebook   A type of portable or mobile computer, sometimes called a laptop.

online banking   The ability to perform banking activities online, typically at a bank's secure website.

phishing   A type of scam that extracts personal information from the victim using a series of fake emails and websites.

photo-sharing site   A website where users can upload, store, and share digital photographs with other users.

Pinterest   Launched in March 2010, a visual social network. Users "pin" interesting images on virtual boards, which are then shared with online friends and followers.

Post Office Protocol (POP) One technology used to send email over the Internet via dedicated email servers; POP email requires the use of special email client software.

private browsing A mode of anonymous web browsing in which no record is kept of the sites you visit.

profile page On a social network, this displays a user's personal information.

router A piece of equipment that connects all the computers on a network; wireless networks use wireless routers.

Safari The web browser included with Apple computers, smartphones, and tablets.

search engine This scours the Web to create an index of web pages that can then be searched by users.

second-level domain The part of a web address between the two "dots." Most second-level domains identify the host company or organization. For example, in the URL www.quepublishing.com, **quepublishing** is the second-level domain.

secure server This encrypts your credit card information and provides a safe online shopping experience.

server A computer connected to the Internet that serves information and services to users.

shopping cart A virtual one of these holds the items you purchase at an online store.

Skype One of the most popular video chatting services, owned by Microsoft.

smartphone A mobile phone with advanced computer-like capability, typically including Internet access and the ability to run task-specific apps.

social media Websites, services, and platforms that people use to share experiences and opinions with each other. The most common social media include social networks, social bookmarking services, and microblogs.

social network A website, such as Facebook or LinkedIn, where users can form communities with like-minded people and share details of their lives with friends, family, fellow students, and coworkers.

spider   Software used by search engines to crawl the Web with the goal of finding and indexing websites.

spyware   A type of malicious software that installs itself on your computer and surreptitiously sends information about the way you use your PC to a third party.

status update   A short post from a member of a social networking site, conveying the user's current thoughts, actions, and such.

streaming audio and video   These let you listen to music and watch movies in real time without first downloading the complete file to your computer.

subdomain   The part of a web address between the http:// and the first "dot." Often **www**, for World Wide Web.

tabbed browsing   Lets you open multiple web pages within a single browser window, with each page displayed on its own tab.

TCP/IP   For *Transmission Control Protocol/Internet Protocol*, the networking technology that manages data transmission and communications between Internet servers.

thread   A collection of messages and replies about a given topic.

top-level domain   The part of a web address after the second "dot" that identifies the type of organization hosting the website. Common top-level domains include **com** (commercial), **org** (nonprofit organization), **edu** (education), and **gov** (government).

tweet   A short, 140-character post on the Twitter social media network. Also used as a verb, "to tweet."

Twitter   A popular microblogging service, launched in 2006, where users post short text messages ("tweets") of no more than 140 characters, which other users can then follow.

uniform resource locator (URL)   The full address of a website or server, including the protocol identifier and the resource name.

video chat   A real-time, face-to-face chat between two people, using their computers or smartphones and built-in cameras or webcams.

viral   Achieving immense popularity via word of mouth on the Internet.

Web   Short for *World Wide Web*.

web-based application   An application housed on and run from computers connected to the Internet; you access web-based applications using your computer's web browser via any Internet connection.

web-based email   Sends and receives email over the Web using any web browser.

web browser   A software program that enables you to access the Web and display specific web pages. Popular web browsers include Microsoft Edge, Internet Explorer, Mozilla Firefox, Google Chrome, and Apple's Safari.

web page   A single document on the Web, typically housed on a website.

web server   A computer that hosts one or more websites.

webcam   A small camera that attaches to your computer and records video, audio, and still pictures. The word "webcam" also refers to hardware webcams connected to the Internet that stream continuous images or video to other computer users.

website   An organized collection of pages on the Web.

Wi-Fi   The 802.11x wireless networking standard used in home and public networks.

Wikipedia   An online encyclopedia with content written and edited by the site's users.

World Wide Web   A collection of linked websites and pages hosted on servers connected to the Internet.

YouTube   The Internet's largest video-sharing community, where members upload and view millions of video files each day.

zombie computer   A computer that has been hijacked by a virus or spyware and used to attack another computer by remote control.

Index

J-K

L

X-Y

Z

More Best-Selling **My** Books!

Learning to use your smartphone, tablet, camera, game, or software has never been easier with the full-color My Series. You'll find simple, step-by-step instructions from our team of experienced authors. The organized, task-based format allows you to quickly and easily find exactly what you want to achieve.

Visit quepublishing.com/mybooks to learn more.

REGISTER THIS PRODUCT
SAVE 35%*
ON YOUR NEXT PURCHASE!

How to Register Your Product

- Go to quepublishing.com/register
- Sign in or create an account
- Enter the 10- or 13-digit ISBN that appears on the back cover of your product

Benefits of Registering

- Ability to download product updates
- Access to bonus chapters and workshop files
- A 35% coupon to be used on your next purchase – valid for 30 days
  - To obtain your coupon, click on "Manage Codes" in the right column of your Account page
- Receive special offers on new editions and related Que products

Please note that the benefits for registering may vary by product. Benefits will be listed on your Account page under Registered Products.

We value and respect your privacy. Your email address will not be sold to any third party company.

* 35% discount code presented after product registration is valid on most print books, eBooks, and full-course videos sold on QuePublishing.com. Discount may not be combined with any other offer and is not redeemable for cash. Discount code expires after 30 days from the time of product registration. Offer subject to change.

quepublishing.com